This book is dedicated to my beautiful daughters, Jacqueline, Victoria and Olivia and my wonderful husband Dennis. I love you.

Acknowledgements:

Writing this book has been an incredible journey. The thoughts and emotions I felt during some of the most difficult and some of the happiest times in my life, somehow found their way onto the pages of this book. I couldn't have done it without the love and support of the incredible people in my life.

To my beautiful children Jacqueline, Victoria & Olivia: God gave me the greatest gifts in life when I became your mother. What matters most is that we hold onto hope, find the fight inside and keep moving forward even on days when it's the hardest thing to do. We are blessed because we have each other. I wish you the ability to see yourselves through my eyes because you have incredible souls that shine from within. I wish you a lifetime of love, laughter and light. I love you all more than I could ever put into words.

To my husband Dennis: You came into my life and helped bring back laughter, faith, hope and love. You became the calm in my stormy days until the light once again appeared. Thank you for believing in me and helping me to once again believe in myself. I am grateful, thankful and feel truly blessed for the love we share. I look forward to continuing on this journey of life by your side always. I love you.

To my mother Arleen: You are one of the strongest women I know. Thank you for always being an amazing example of love, strength, honor and grace. I don't know what I would do without you in my life.

To my father John: Thank you for being an incredible example of strength and for always being a proud daddy. You always made me feel that I could accomplish anything.

To my sister Erika: I'm definitely thankful that God gave me a sister. We have always been each other's biggest supporters. We will continue to support each other no matter what this life throws our way. I'm thankful also that when you were little, I could bribe you to secrecy with just a Happy Meal from McDonald's. Thank you for giving me my first and only beautiful niece Brooklynn Sofia and nephew on the way! We are very blessed with a beautiful family.

To my Stepfather Rick, aka G-Rick (Grampy): Thank you for always being there and for the support you have shown since the day you became part of our lives.

To my brother-in-law Steve: You were an incredible support during the most difficult of times. That is something I will not ever forget. Thank you.

Friends: "Friends are the family that you choose for yourself."

I have some of the most incredible friends in this life. I don't know where I would be without them. Through the happiest of times to the most tragic of times your friendship and support has been a gift. From my junior high school/high-school friends that I am beyond thankful to still remain friends with today, to the friends I have made on this life's journey, to the friends that I could call at 3am and you would be there. You know who you are & I love you all!

To my co-author Paul Lonardo: I'm thankful that our paths crossed and you could help me tell my story. I only hope that somehow my story will help others realize how important it is to keep moving forward even if it's one small step at a time while holding onto faith, love & hope.

In Memory of Michael A. Passaretti

"Forever with the Angels Always in our hearts"

1968-2015

Michael, although your life on this earth was short, the impact you made on your family

and everyone that was blessed enough to have known and loved you was enormous.

Your memory and legacy will live on especially within our beautiful children.

List of Chapters

Chapter 1 **THE BEGINNING**

"True love stories never have endings." ~ Richard Bach

Michael had a caring and loving nature. He was someone who laughed and joked and had an infectious personality that everyone was drawn to, especially me. After we got married, he became an incredible husband and family man and then the best loving and devoted dad to our three daughters. He was actively involved in their upbringing, from changing diapers to helping them with their homework. He was the softball coach of our daughters' teams and everyone in the community adored him. Michael loved his family more than anything else. He enjoyed his work and just loved life. Always easy-going, he lived his life by the philosophy, "don't sweat the small stuff." He was never violent, rarely even raised his voice, and I can't remember ever having anything approaching an argument, even when we disagreed on something.

This personality portrait of Michael, right through to the last two weeks of his life, was the Michael I knew, the Michael everyone knew. He was the last person anyone, not just I, could ever imagine would commit suicide. The loss of a spouse and the absence of my daughters' father from their lives is hard enough, but this incongruous act added profoundly to my grief as I searched for an answer why.

I was eighteen the first time I heard of Michael. I was with my 12-year old sister, on our way to church. My mother would typically take us each week but this day she wasn't feeling well. She did, however, make sure she used her "Italian mother's way" of coercing us to get off to church without her. My father wasn't much of a churchgoer, however, he was supportive of our Catholic upbringing and was spiritual in his own way which included paying for our Catholic education. The pot of meatballs and gravy was on the stove simmering as she told us to "hurry up" because we were going to be late. As practicing Catholics,

1

we were not allowed to eat anything before Mass. It was practically a sacramental law, never to eat before receiving the Eucharist. We would leave the house, which was permeated with the smell of Sunday dinner with our stomachs rumbling. All I could think about was getting back home to eat. It was always tempting to rip off a piece of Italian bread while dunking it into the pot of gravy on the way out the door, risking the prospect of eternal damnation in the process.

As my sister and I reached the parking lot, the church bells were ringing, and I can still recall our conversation. We started talking about a boy she liked. She would see at middle school dances and they would talk on the phone all the time. I believe they were scheming a plan to fix me up with the boy's uncle, Michael. I was not interested, because I was already in a relationship. When my sister hinted that he was a bit of a "player" and said he dated a lot, I *really* wasn't interested. I told her to forget it, however jokingly said "If he met me, he would fall under my spell and madly in love and that would be it." My sister gave me the major eyeroll and said "Yeah, yeah, I know." But that wasn't the end of it.

While my sister continued seeing and talking to Michael's nephew, she didn't mention fixing Michael up with me again until about a year later. By then, the relationship that I was in had ended. One day my sister asked me for a ride to a dance she was going to with Michael's nephew and a group of kids. They all met at the nephew's grandfather's house which just so happened to be where Michael also lived.

TIMING IS EVERYTHING

I remember it was a cold January night in 1993. I pulled up to the house and my sister begged me to go inside with her. She told me she wanted me to meet the grandfather. She said he was an incredible man. He turned out to be all that and more, but I knew he wasn't the only person she wanted me to meet. I was sitting at the table when Michael's father walked in. He had amazing energy. He was all of 5'5, very Italian and loud but in a fun, loving way. Basically, he was everything I was used to

2

growing up. He made me feel at home. As I was sitting at the kitchen table, Michael came up from downstairs. I remember seeing him and thinking that he had the same energy as his father. He had just come from the gym, and he was wearing sweats and a baseball hat turned backwards on his head. We sat together at the table and I completely lost track of time. I hadn't realized that my sister had gone off to the dance with her friends, and the next thing I knew an hour had passed as I talked with Michael about pretty much everything under the sun. I told him was that I was going to college full-time and also working two jobs. One was in retail because I loved getting discounts on the clothes, and the other was as a waitress in a restaurant.

The major topic we discussed, which turned out to be a pivotal moment in our burgeoning relationship, was about the upcoming Super Bowl. While I wasn't really a sports fan, I did grow up in a diehard New York Yankee baseball family. Michael being a diehard Red Sox fan always made for some interesting and fun-loving rivalry in our household through the years. Even our children became divided with one becoming a Yankee fan and our other two Red Sox fans. Michael mentioned that he and his friends always bet on the Super Bowl, and that year he bet $500 on the Buffalo Bills, who were playing the Dallas Cowboys. I was in shock! I couldn't imagine having $500 to just "play with" but he thought it was fun and made the game more interesting for him.

When I finally got up to leave, Michael told me that he would love to take me out sometime., He gave me his home number. This was before the days when everyone had cell phones. He wasn't pushy, and he understood that I had a lot going on between school and work. Well, I didn't call him right away. I was nineteen years old and believed that playing a little "hard to get" was always the best policy.

The night of the Super Bowl I was working, but I could hear the guys in the kitchen yelling or cheering loudly. "Hey, who won?" I asked one of the guys when the game was over. When I heard that it wasn't the team Michael had bet on, my jaw dropped. "Oh my God!" I thought. Michael had just lost $500! I felt terrible about it, and I did what any sweet, sensitive girl would do upon hearing news like that; I called him when I got home to offer my sympathies. He picked up on the first ring.

"Hello." He sounded tired and drained of energy, and he clearly did not know it was me.

"So, are you going to be betting on any more games in the near future?" I said like a lecturing mother.

Immediately, he starts laughing. "I can't believe it. She doesn't call me for two weeks and then calls me to bust me up."

They say timing is everything, and between the Super Bowl and playing hard to get, it all worked out, setting into motion the start of a wonderful life together, a twenty-year marriage and a beautiful family.

FIRST DATE

Soon after that phone call, we made plans to go out on our first date, which turned out to be a story of its own that we would laugh about every time it was brought up.

Again, this was a time before cellphones or GPS, and although I lived only about twenty minutes from Michael, it was an area that was very rural, and at night with no street lights it was very dark. We made plans to eat at a restaurant that ironically would be in the same town we would call home years later and the place that I call home today. Well, I got all dressed up and was waiting in anxious anticipation for Michael to arrive. I kept looking out the window every time a car approached but each time it just went by the house. As it got later and later, I began to pace around the room and my Italian temper started to flare.

How dare he stand me up!

I even started yelling at my sister. "I TOLD you that I didn't want to go out with him from the beginning!"

Just then there was a knock at the door. My mother answered it and as soon as she opened the door Michael began

4

apologizing profusely for being so late.

"Can I use your phone," he asked, telling my mother that he wanted to call his father to tell him that he made it.

This was something that had a big impact on my mother and me. Even though he was twenty-four years old, Michael was still his father's baby. I found that endearing. His father was his best friend. His mother sadly passed from cancer in 1986 at the age of fifty-two.

He was the youngest of three boys but both of his brothers were more than ten years older than he. He used to jokingly call himself an "Oops" baby.

My mother immediately fell in love with Michael. The fact that he wanted to call his father, who he knew would be worried, earned him "major points" with my mom. I came down to greet him after he had gotten off the phone. He began to apologize to me, saying over and over again how sorry he was for getting lost and not leaving his house earlier than he had.

"Don't worry about it," my mother said, granting him complete absolution. "I'm sure she gave you confusing directions."

"Wait? What? Me?" Little did I know that this would be the way the next twenty-two years would go. It was actually very humorous. Whenever something went wrong, no matter what it was, it was never Michael's fault, at least in the eyes of my mother. It was just one of the things I would have to accept during our life together, and I gladly did.

As Michael and I were leaving the house to go on our first date, albeit quite late, he walked through the door ahead of me. I followed behind him, but before I left, I turned to look at my mother, as I would do when I went out on a date with a boy that I was unsure about. I would look at her and either give her a nod and a smile, or I would give her the "finger across the throat sign." This meant I would be home in an hour but this time we both looked at each other and smiled.

GETTING ENGAGED

What happened *after* our first date I would describe only as a whirlwind. We were together every single day. He made me laugh and smile, and I felt that way every time I was with him. He also made me feel protected and safe. It was exhilarating. I was so swept off my feet that by Memorial Day, just four months later, we were engaged.

That holiday weekend, we were at my uncle's house for a party. Family and friends were all around as we went inside to watch a playoff game between the Chicago Bulls and the New York Knicks. It was fitting that our engagement involved some type of sporting event. Michael had gotten me into watching all types of sports. I was really getting into the basketball game when I felt him take my left hand and take the ring that I was wearing off my finger. It was a really pretty gold ring that had been given to me by Michael's father. The man was always so incredibly giving like that, and I knew he loved Michael and I together from the first day.

The next thing I knew Michael was looking me in the eyes and saying, "You know that I loved you from the first day I met you. I know we talked about the future and getting married someday. How about we make it official?"

I was actually watching the basketball game pretty intently when he said all this to me, and when he paused awaiting my response, I nonchalantly said, "Okay, sure," without turning away from the game.

"Look at your hand," he said, and I glanced down quickly but immediately looked back up at the television. "*Look good!*" he said with more urgency, and when I did, I saw this shiny diamond ring on my hand and I realized what was happening.

The moment I became fully aware, I saw members of my family coming all around us with cameras clicking. At that moment, the party was instantly transformed into our engagement party. It was a really amazing time. We defied everyone who said, "No way this would work." Those would be the people that didn't really know us. I suppose on the outside looking in its easy to judge something like that. Here's a couple who had only known each other for four months. I was nineteen-years old and he was twenty-four. We get engaged. What business do we have getting engaged? If people had placed bets on the odds of us not staying together, they surely would have lost as badly as the Bills did in the Super Bowl XXVII. We may have been the underdogs in many eyes, but soon they would all see our relationship blossom into a true love story written for the ages.

Chapter 2   **THE DAY OUR WORLD CRASHED**

I stirred and woke to the sight of a grainy silhouette in the corner of my bedroom. It was dark and I was half asleep, but I knew it was Michael. He was standing near the bureau on his side of the bed with his back towards me. I glanced at the clock. It was 4 a.m. I looked back at my husband, who remained standing quiet and motionless.

"Michael, we're going to see a doctor today," I said, trying to keep my voice from trembling. "Okay?" He didn't respond. By this point, after about ten days of unusual behavior, I knew that something was clearly wrong with Michael's mental state, and I was beyond concerned. It all happened so fast. Thinking back on some of the events over the previous week and a half, it was clear to me that Michael's slow downward spiral into some unknown psychosis had left him delusional, paranoid and frighteningly unpredictable. Each day it was as if the Michael I had known for more than twenty years was slipping away, and a stranger, an imposter who was different in every way, had taken his place.

I did not see what was happening at first because Michael had always been so strong mentally and physically. To me and our three girls, he was a tower of strength, our protector. He often told me, "In this life, nothing else matters as long as we all have our health and each other." Suddenly, he didn't seem to have either. I was far from a weak person myself, but he only made me stronger. If one of us was down, the other was there for support and strength.

The man who was standing with his back to me in the darkness of our bedroom that night was a very different person. For a person whose personal belief had always been 'never sweat the small stuff,' suddenly he would become overly fixated on trivial matters that never would have bothered him before, not EVER. This was the day it finally hit me that he was not getting better and I needed to do something. He needed help, and I was determined that this would be the day that we would address whatever problems he was having. I may not have had any idea what was happening to him or why, but there had to be someone who could help us figure it out.

The next thing I heard was the sound of the front door closing. "Michael," I said in a soft, comforting tone, but he was gone. It was as if he had evaporated in front of me. I turned to look back at the clock and it was 5 a.m. I had intended to get up with him when I first saw him standing there, but I must have fallen back to sleep. I quickly reached for my cell phone on the nightstand next to my bed and texted Michael.

Where you going?

A moment later, I heard the beep of his cell phone from the kitchen as my text was received. I instantly jumped out of bed and went to the kitchen to find his wallet along with his phone on the counter. He never went anywhere without these items. This made no sense to me. I told myself to stay calm, but I was scared. When I looked out the kitchen window, I saw him sitting in his car in the driveway. He was shrouded in the glow of the vehicle's interior light. I raced to my closet and threw on the first pair of shoes I could find before going outside to see what he was doing, but by then it was too late; the car was gone. Now I was really scared, not knowing where he was going or what his intentions might be. I went back upstairs to get dressed and try to figure out what was going on and what I should do. My head was in a fog as I walked into the bedroom. I took two steps inside and stopped when I noticed that the drawer to Michael's bureau, which he had been standing in front of earlier, was opened slightly. The sinking feeling in my gut became full on nausea as I stepped over to the drawer and saw the box where Michael kept a handgun. He had a permit for the weapon, which he had purchased for our protection fifteen years earlier, and kept it in a locked box in the drawer. Now the box was unlocked and the gun was gone. I almost didn't see the note next to the box, but as soon as I spotted it, I grasped it. Holding it in trembling hands, I read the words with a furrowed brow. It was written in a very cryptic manner, the handwriting barely recognizable as Michael's.

9

His message was short and direct, telling our daughters and me that he loved us with everything in him but he wasn't ok and God would save him.

At that moment, it felt as if the whole world was spinning out of control.

What was I reading? What was happening? What do I do?

TODAY TOMORROW FOREVER

My daughters Victoria, 16, and Olivia, 11, were both asleep in their rooms and would be getting up soon. Michael was supposed to take Olivia to school that morning. Our oldest daughter, Jackie, was a freshman in college, living in Boston.

I went into panic mode, worrying about my girls and what I was going to tell them when they woke up. I still had no idea what was really happening. As the line between reality and the surreal continued to blur, I wished this was all some overly vivid nightmare from which I would soon awaken. Unsure what else to do, I called my sister. Despite the early hour of the morning, she picked up right away, knowing I wouldn't have called her at that time if it wasn't an emergency.

I told her what was happening and asked her to come over right away. I could always count on my sister whenever I needed her. We had always been close and would do anything for one another. She got there as soon as she could to help me with the girls. They were told that I had to take their father to the doctor because of the knee pain he had recently been experiencing. It was at least a lie they would believe because Michael had been out of work due to the injury.

I also called my father because I needed someone to drive around with me looking for Michael. I knew I couldn't drive because I could barely feel my legs. I needed to find my husband. My mother, who has always been my rock, was away on vacation in South Carolina.

I kept saying to myself, *"Michael where did you go?"* The

10

first place we went was the gym where Michael worked out every day. When he wasn't there, we tried the park near the house where he grew up. There was an outside chance that we would find him at the park, though I knew in my heart that he wouldn't be there, either. He wasn't.

My anxiety level shot up, my heartrate pounding like a drum in my chest. It occurred to me to call a friend I had grown up with who was now a police officer. Barely able to breathe as I spoke to him, I explained the situation and he offered his help. He asked me to give him some ideas of other places that Michael might have gone and people he might seek out. It was hard to think, but I gave him a list of addresses of friends, family and possible locations he might be. My friend promised me that several police officers would be dispatched to go out and look for Michael. I was so grateful and hopeful that they would find him.

I was asked if Michael had a gun with him.

Oh my God how do I answer this? "We do own a gun legally but I'm not sure if he has it with him." I wasn't completely honest. I knew it was wrong, but I was just trying to protect Michael. I was totally certain that he wasn't out there looking to hurt anyone, but I didn't want him to get hurt, either. I was thinking, *Please, just find him, and he will realize that things will be ok.*

However, despite all the places that my friend and the police were looking, there was no trace of Michael. Then out of the blue, a vision of St. Ann's Cemetery came into my mind. It was where both Michael's parents were buried, but beyond that I cannot explain what made me think of it. His mother had passed away when he was 17-years old, which happened to be the same age as our oldest daughter, Jackie. His father had passed two months before our wedding. As much as he loved his parents, Michael almost never went to the cemetery. He felt that when people died, they were always with you everywhere, not just at a cemetery. However, something inside made me think that he had gone there now.

Thinking about it later, I reasoned that my intuition may

have had something to do with a ring belonging to his father that Michael had starting wearing on a gold chain around his neck. He wore the ring alongside a medallion of St. Michael which I had bought for him on our first wedding anniversary. The inscription on the back of the medallion read; *Michael and Janine, Today, Tomorrow, Forever.* I remember asking him why he was wearing his father's ring, and I don't think I got a straight answer. However, at the time he was up for a big position at the company where he had been working for over twenty-five years, and I felt the ring and the medallion were a way to bring him the feeling of having "his angels, more specifically, his mother and father on his side.

SECOND-GUESSING

Had this been the onset of when things started to change for him? Should I have paid more attention to this than I had? Was he recognizing that something was happening inside him and he needed protection? Was that something that I should have picked up on?

The change in Michael's personality and mental state was so sudden that it was as if someone had flipped a switch. I remember we were watching Jackie's college softball game in Boston, enjoying seeing her get her first hit as a freshman and make her first defensive play in centerfield, when Michael got a phone call. That call seemed to have triggered the start of his peculiar behavior and thought processes. He became distant and began fidgeting with hands, when just mere minutes before, he was totally in the moment and he and I were cheering on Jackie. This would be the beginning of what I called the "days in hell" and the last time Jackie would set foot on a softball field in a college uniform.

Michael and I, being very spiritual, believed that there was a reason for everything that happens on this earth, and we often had deep discussions about this and related topics. We always had a clear understanding of the way the other was thinking, and now, I was out trying to find Michael by making some sense of what was happening in his mind. Nothing could

12

have been further from my mind than the possibility he would take himself permanently away from our girls and me.

I can recall one of the days we were having one of our deep conversations reflecting on our life. This day we were sitting by the water.

"Michael, how are we still this good after so many years? I believe that this life is supposed to be a lesson and that when we have learned our lesson it's done. Sometimes it's a little scary to me because I feel that we 'get it.' We value our life, our relationship, our family. Instead of growing apart or complacent, we keep growing together, stronger. We know what's important. I hope that God doesn't take one of us out of this equation because we have it *too good.* I feel like life isn't fair and just when you think you have it altogether something comes to shake that all up."

"Don't think like that." he told me. "Each day is a gift. We have things that money can't buy. Some people can have all the money in the world and yet are not happy. We have all the things that matter the most. That's the thing that we always need to remember. We have to remember to not sweat the small stuff."

This is something Michael always said to me, something I will always remember. Eerily, I recall that conversation often and so many others that we had that were based on our ideals, values and views of life that Michael would have never ended of his own doing.

I was still driving in the car with my father when I phoned my mother. My parents had been divorced since I was nineteen, and my mother later remarried. I cannot recall her exact words that confusing and dreadful day, but I know that she did what any mother who loves her children would do; she stayed strong, even if she was falling apart on the inside herself. Earlier while we were driving, I texted her; *I am in hell right now.* Hauntingly, this would be something that I would be feeling for a very long time after that day.

Suddenly, I said out loud that I thought Michael may be at

13

the cemetery. I could no longer deny the vision and feeling I had that he had gone there. I couldn't remember his parent's plot number, however, so my dad drove us all around the cemetery, but to no avail. We were just ready to take a left onto a road that would have taken us to a different part of the cemetery, and to Michael, but my police officer friend called asking me to meet him and a detective back at my house. We never took that left, and it is something that will haunt me to this day, wondering what the outcome might have been if we had.

I had no idea what I was being summoned home for, but I had an uneasy feeling as we drove home in complete silence. Upon my fretful return home with my father, my friend was waiting for me. A detective and several other officers were also there, with no news about Michael's whereabouts. One of them asked me if they could search Michael's drawers in my bedroom. I allowed them to do so, knowing full well what they would find. I didn't try to hide the empty gun box, which they found right away. They continued talking in hushed tones amongst themselves and communicating with other officers who were still out searching for Michael.

WHEN THE UNIMAGINABLE HAPPENS

Shortly thereafter, the detective asked to speak with me in private, and proceeded to ask me a bunch of different questions in an attempt to get to the bottom of why Michael would take his gun and leave the house. I showed him the note Michael left me and said that even though he hadn't been himself of late, none of this could be further from his character.

The next thing I knew I was just pacing around the kitchen and living room waiting for someone to say they had found him, and that they were bringing him home. In my mind, I believed that this was how it would play out, and once he was home, I would take him to get the help that he needed, and everything would be fine.

All of a sudden there was a buzz and a lot of activity among the police offers. I overheard them saying the Michael had been found. He was at the cemetery, at his mother and father's gravesite, sitting in his car. My sister and my mother's best friend, Mary, who had recently arrived and would remain by my side for the duration of what was to come, were both crying and hugging me, saying, "Thank God!" I, however, didn't have the same reaction. I was still numb. Something inside me knew it wasn't right. I looked my friend in the eyes.

"He's still in his car?" I asked.

"Yes."

We were both thinking the same thing. He told me that they were communicating with him.

Communicating? What did that mean? I just wanted to go to him, but they would not let me.

Waiting for any additional news seemed like an eternity, when suddenly I heard the front door open and turned to see several uniformed officers and the detective that I spoke with earlier step inside. The looks on their faces were not what I had been hoping and praying to God to see. They kept me in their sights, but none of them would look me directly in the eye. I turned to my police officer friend for some answers. He looked at me sympathetically before he approached me. Bracing a hand on my shoulder, he said, "Janine, he shot himself. I'm so sorry."

I heard the words he spoke, but it was as if someone was speaking to me in another language. They had no meaning. It made no sense. Michael could never have done such a thing. I was still trying to process the meaning of these words when a tremendous ringing pierced my ears and my legs gave out. I dropped to the floor screaming uncontrollable. I had no control over my body. If there was anything I remember at that moment with any clarity, it was our three -month-old puppy, Sonny, jumping on me. He did not want to play, but seemed to sense something was wrong, and he wanted to be with me. The next thing I knew I was sitting in the back seat of the detective's car with my sister being driven to the hospital to see Michael. I didn't know if he was alive or dead. My sister was crying and praying and holding onto me. I was numb. I wasn't feeling anything, I wasn't thinking, and I wasn't moving. I didn't know it, but I was in shock. I was in the middle of some dark recess somewhere in my mind trying to process the reality that I was actually on the way to a hospital to see my husband who shot himself.

He shot himself?

He shot himself?

I kept hearing these words repeated over and over in my head. No matter how many times I said it to myself, I could not believe it. There was no way that my husband, the father of our three beautiful daughters, our protector, and the strong, funny, happy, healthy man that I married would ever take his own life. Not in a million lifetimes. Besides, God wouldn't take him from us like that, I kept thinking. Whatever happened, it was just a misunderstanding, and he would be all right. He will come home and we will get him the help he needs. That's what I believed. That's what I had to believe.

When we arrived at the hospital, my sister and I were taken into a small, private room with the detective. Within a few minutes, several doctors joined us. I felt like I was watching a dramatic scene in some daytime soap opera instead of taking part in this real-life horror. Everything was happening in slow motion as one of the doctors stepped forward and made her way over to me. She looked me in the eyes, paused a moment, and said, "I'm so sorry. He didn't make it."

No! No, no, no, no, no. There has been some kind of mistake. Michael was fine last night. And he is okay now. We just need to get him the help he needs.

These were the fragmented thoughts that were rampaging through my brain, but I couldn't manage to utter a single word. My sister reacted with a wail, crying very loudly and holding me tightly. Michael had been like a brother to her since she was twelve years old. She was the one who brought us together twenty-three years earlier.

The world began spinning around me once again, faster

than before, and I didn't think it was ever going to stop. It was like being inside a tornado with my life swirling around me, and my sister was trying to keep me from flying off. I just needed to see my husband, but before I could say anything I was taken into the room where Michael was lying lifeless with a tube in his mouth. He looked like he was just sleeping, as if any minute he would wake up. He didn't, and I didn't wake up from this nightmare.

I don't remember calling my father, who came down immediately, while my mother got on the next flight home from South Carolina. I remained with Michael, holding his hand. It was surreal, and all the while I couldn't help hoping that at some point, he would just open his eyes, and everything would be okay.

Then it occurred to me that I had to tell our three beautiful daughters that their father was gone. How was I supposed to do that?

Dear God, give me strength!

I stepped into the waiting area to call my eldest daughter's boyfriend at the time. He happened to be with his parents when he answered. I asked to speak to his mother rather than tell him directly what happened. They were all very close with us, and I just told her to get to the hospital, that it wasn't good. All of them came right down, joining many of my family members who began to assemble to be by my side. It was comforting to have so much support around me when the horrible news was broken to my daughters. They needed everyone who loved them to help them through this. I needed them, too, and I felt fortunate to come from a large, loving family, beginning with my mother who had five sisters and three brothers. I would lean on them to help carry me through this debilitating sorrow that was only just beginning.

I still had to get my eldest daughter home from Boston, and I didn't know how I was going to do that without telling her why. It was not easy and it required me to put on the biggest act of my life, but somehow, I was able to keep it together as I spoke

17

to her. I asked her to trust me, insisting that she just needed to come home, and she did without question. She was on the next train home. My other daughters were with my mother's best friend, who would bring them to my mother's house when we got there. Once this was all arranged, I just collapsed on the floor of the hospital hallway, screaming on the top of my lungs. I knew I had to say goodbye to Michael.

This cannot be my life!

Please God, let me wake up from this nightmare!

I went back inside Michael's room and held his hand. The last time I would have my hand inside of his. I kissed his forehead. Letting go of his hand for the last time was the hardest thing I ever had to do. At that moment, I walked away from my husband forever, leaving behind my best friend, the father of my children, the man I loved more than anything. The wonderful, loving, comfortable life that the girls and I had come to know was shattered. Nothing would ever be the same.

WHEN THE LAST BELL RANG

I was physically and emotionally drained, unsure how I was even functioning as I dragged myself from the hospital to my mother's house. I wanted to collapse when I walked through the door, but I knew my daughters would be there shortly. My cousin, who is a priest, had been at the hospital, and was with me for emotional and spiritual support. If the girls had any clue that something was really wrong from my cousin's presence, they did not let on. However, when everyone began to arrive at the house all at once, practically our entire family, consisting of aunts, uncles, cousins and some close family friends, they knew something extremely bad had happened. The anguish I felt deep within my soul as I looked into these innocent, frightened faces that were peering intently at me for answers was heartbreaking enough, but then I had to tell them that their dad was gone. It was something that will forever be ingrained into my mind and my darkest nightmares. The words came out. There was no gentle way to put it. If there was, I didn't know what it was.

I wanted to hold my daughters and take *their* pain away. The cries for their father and the tortured screams that came from them as they all dropped to the floor in anguish and pain was too much for me to bear.

What do I do? How can I help my daughters? How can I make this pain stop?

There wasn't a thing I could do. NOT A THING.

My entire body went limp and my legs gave out as I fell helplessly to the floor while watching the agonized faces of my beautiful innocent children. The only thing I could do was sob uncontrollably.

Inevitably, the dreaded question came about; how did he die? It didn't make sense to me, so I didn't know how I could make them understand that their father had killed himself. They wouldn't believe it, nor would they accept it. I made the decision that night that no one was to tell Olivia. She was only eleven, and she couldn't possibly handle news or understand the reasons behind her father's action. I wanted to protect her, so she wouldn't find out the truth until much later. I tried to explain to Jackie and Victoria that something went wrong in his mind, and he wasn't himself when he did it. There was no way that their dad would ever have taken his own life and taken himself away from us if he was in his right mind.

The task of preparing for Michael's funeral was torturous. I don't know how I made it through that week, but I know that I couldn't have done it without my family. So many people came to visit, or send food and flowers. They really wanted to show my girls and me their support and love.

I couldn't help but feel like I was in the middle of someone else's life. The numbness that invaded my body spread, penetrating deep within me. I couldn't eat. I couldn't sleep. When I did manage to close my eyes for a brief a time, I would wake to either my own cries or the cries of my daughters. It was a feeling of complete despair and helplessness not being able to provide the girls with the comfort they needed, or anything that would take away the pain they were feeling.

I did not want to fall asleep because I always woke up with the hope in my mind that it was all a terrible nightmare, but then I would realize that it was real and I would be ambushed by such dread, a suffocating profound sadness, that I could not find the strength to get out of bed or function in any way for hours.

I needed a lot of support and the strength of the Heavens the day I went to the funeral home to make the arrangements. I had to look at the choice of urns and pick one for the placement of Michael's ashes as part of the fulfillment of his wishes to be cremated. My uncles came with me and helped me with that task. I asked them to choose something that they thought would be good and show me because I couldn't bear to walk through an array of urns and caskets. They presented me with pictures of a few urns they selected, and I picked one. The photo of Michael that I chose for the funeral was one with him watching his daughters swim in the ocean on Block Island. It was one of my favorite photos of him. It captured him doing what he loved most; being with his family. Amy, one of my best friends, had the photo enlarged for me and put into a beautiful frame with a stand. It took my breath away when I saw it for several reasons.

Decisions, decisions, decisions. That was all it seemed I was doing as I geared up for the day my children and I would "march into hell" together.

Then, a couple of days before the wake, my family was all gathered at my mother's house, where my girls and I were staying, and all I kept hearing about was how long and arduous the wake was going to be and how we would be standing there greeting hundreds of people for four straight hours. Michael was forty-six years old, and he had so many friends and people who knew him and our family. They would all come to pay their respects, and suddenly I began to doubt if my children and I could handle all that. We were barely getting by each day as it was. I thought about this for a while, and then walked out of my mother's living room crying while saying that we needed to call off the wake. I decided I wanted it to be private, only for close friends and family the morning of his funeral. There was no way that I could endure to see the girls in any more pain, especially if it was something that I could shield them from. If I could, in my limited power, protect them from any additional trauma, I should do it.

As we arrived at the church the morning of the funeral, I saw that the pews on both sides were filled, many standing in the back of the church because there were no seats. I couldn't believe the number of people that were there. Besides our family, there were friends, coworkers, teachers, teammates, coaches and parents from every softball team my daughters played on. Some friends who I hadn't seen in years were sitting among the congregation, showing their admiration and love not only for Michael, but also for my children and me. It actually made me gasp for air. My girls and I held each other as we proceeded down the church aisle.

To say this ceremony was difficult was an understatement. It was like having a knife plunged into our hearts as we sat and listened to the service led by my cousin, the priest. At one point, the sun was shining through the stained-glass window directly onto Michael's picture, which had been placed on the top of the altar. To me this was a sign that Michael was there that day, and would always be there, watching over us.

The tormented cries of my daughters that day is something that will stay in my mind forever. Throughout the service, we held each other up, literally and figuratively, and we continue to do so today.

After the funeral liturgy concluded, we walked out of the church arm in arm. As we proceeded outside into the courtyard area, I began to hear the somber, melodious chime of the church bells. The sound instantly brought me back to a time when I was nine years-old, sitting in the schoolyard at the end of my grandmother's street. I would go there by myself when school was out and bring a book to read on lazy summer days. I always loved to read, and I would spend hours there reading, consumed by the words that seemed to be written just for me and getting lost in my own thoughts. When I would hear the peal of church bells ring out from the church down the street, I knew it was lunchtime. I would look up and smile as I listened to the chimes echoing through the warm air. It was beautiful. Magical, somehow. When the last bell rang, I would head back to my grandmother's house, where she would already have lunch made for my sister and me.

Now, thirty years later, I once again heard the familiar and comforting sound of church bells as I was walking out of my husband's funeral mass with our children by my side. It was a very different feeling from the time I recall hearing church bells ringing out at nine years old.

With my girls in tow, I went to stand next to the wall outside the church and I listened as the bells continued to ring. When the last bell rang, I felt as if this was representative of how the life that we had known for so long had come to an abrupt end and another life that we couldn't begin to fathom was just beginning for all of us.

Chapter 3   **A MOTHER'S LOVE**

"A mother is only as happy as her unhappiest child."

There were many challenges facing me as a single mother. Just managing to get through those first few weeks and months after Michael's death was a real struggle. The heartache and unrelenting sadness were all-consuming. We were staying at my mother's house because being on our own was just too much to bear. As it was, some days I didn't even want to get out of bed. How could I do anything when I was walking around feeling like I had a knife in my stomach and struggling to breathe through the pain. When I saw the faces of my girls, however, I knew that they needed me, and I battled every day to come out of this for all of us. The only thing I really wanted was to ensure that my children maintained somewhat of a normal life, even if nothing was normal anymore. We had all known only one way of life, but that had all changed in an instant.

I had one daughter who was away in another state in her first year of college, another daughter in her sophomore year of high school, and my youngest in sixth grade, who were all struggling greatly trying to come to terms with the loss of their father. My daughters and I were so broken. But I had a responsibility to them. I had to be there for them and their needs. I had to be a pillar of strength, and be the one to see them through the most pain that they have ever felt.

Maybe my kids saw me as strong, but the last thing I felt was strong. I had become a machine. I did what I had to do, including looking to move into a new house for the sake of my girls, though I didn't know how I was going to "make a home" again without Michael.

Looking back, I was sleepwalking through those early days after he died. It was like the oxygen was slowly being sucked from my body. All I kept thinking was, *how am I going to get through this and hold everything together?* Michael and I had been a team. We both held it all together. *Together.* That was the

23

key word. I had him as my partner, my source of strength when I was weak, and my best friend since I was nineteen years old. Abruptly he was gone, and I had to do it all by myself.

The burden was crushing. I only managed to get by because of the support system I had. The days after someone dies is like living in a fog. There is constant activity as family and friends do everything that they can to help in any way they can. I was very fortunate to have so many people by my side practically around the clock. There was always someone bringing something to the house. I don't know what I would have done without them.

CHILDREN COPING

Michael's death affected our daughters in different ways. Each of them torturous. I contacted their teachers, guidance counselors, coaches, anyone involved in their academic life, pleading with them to help me support my girls at this time of great suffering. I was thankful because mostly everyone seemed to go above and beyond to embrace them. Jackie's college was very supportive. Her professors gave her the time she needed to be with her family and excused her from many of her assignments. For Jackie, she found that going right back to school and throwing herself into her classes was the best way for her to cope with this tragedy.

My Victoria, who was in 10th grade, also received much-needed support from her high school, especially her softball coaches, who were also her teachers. They would prove to be incredible allies for me for the rest of her high school years. Victoria is the type who keeps things inside, so she had a more difficult time coping as she struggled to hide the massive pain she was suffering. Ironically Victoria's middle name is Hope. At the time I don't think I realized the magnitude that this word/name would be. At the time I remember people asking me why I chose the name Hope. My answer was, *I believe that Hope is something we should always have no matter what hand this life may deal us at times.* Little did I realize how prophetic my answer may have been for my own life.

24

As her mother, I knew what was behind her eyes. I knew my other children the same way. I believe all mothers have an inherent instinct about their children, a way in which we can feel the emotions they are experiencing right along with them, good or bad. We know what's behind the 'mask' they wear for the rest of the world. I just had to be sure Victoria got all the support she needed for as long as she needed it. Whatever I could do within my power.

Then there was my youngest, Olivia. My 11-year-old baby girl had no idea what had happened to her seemingly perfect life. The childhood that she once knew and loved was ripped from her little hands. Her fun loving, happy, joking, caring, protective Daddy was gone. She didn't know the details. I wanted to keep them from her as long as I could. How could she possibly fathom the intricacies of what had been going on in her father's mind that led to him take his own life. I didn't understand what happened myself, so how could I expect such a young girl to grasp it.

How did my older girls process the mystery of what happened to their father?

Although the pain was massive for all of us, Olivia struggled the most, at least outwardly, with her age certainly being the biggest factor. I found myself having to advocate for her at school so much that it shocked me to see just how many people simply could not comprehend the sheer magnitude of what Olivia was dealing with as an eleven-year-old. Some seemed to be under the impression that after a few months had gone by, it had been time enough for her to move on and get back into a "normal routine." Nothing is normal when it comes to grieving, and perhaps the average person does not understand the dynamics of the process. Although most were empathetic, there was an educator at Olivia's school who shockingly, told me, "Its time Olivia learns how to cope."

I have never been a quiet, passive person, especially when it comes to my children and their well-being. When I felt something wasn't right, I would not hesitate to intervene, and I did not take this educator's critique sitting down. "Learn how to cope?" I was an adult and I had a hard enough time trying to figure out how to cope each day. Olivia was a little girl with her world just ripped apart without warning or explanation. It rallied me to take an even firmer stance in the support and defense of all my daughters. If you as a parent aren't going to be the advocates for your children, when they can't advocate for themselves, then who will?

I realized that this was going to be an uphill battle, one that I would sadly fight for quite a while. I arranged multiple meetings with teachers, counselors and administrators. I learned a lot about what people understood about grief. I realized that most did not have much comprehension, if any at all, of the sheer hell we were going through as a family. Grief is very personal, and I didn't expect everyone to completely understand our plight, but what I did expect was some degree of compassion and empathy for my children, and I would desperately fight with everything inside me to ensure they got it.

I made the decision to have Olivia change schools the following school year and attend a small Catholic school in our community. My eldest daughter Jackie had attended the school from 6-8th grade and had a wonderful experience. I realize that each child is different, and it's up to us as parents to try to make decisions for them on an individual basis. What works for one child will not necessarily work for another, so these decisions aren't always easy to make. I have always tried to do what my gut feeling tells me, and this proved to be one of the best decisions I could make for Olivia. It seemed more comforting to her to be in a much smaller environment with smaller classes, and as a consequence she began attending church regularly. I believe she felt a certain level of security in the church, among the clergy, the teachers and the overall environment during this very catastrophic time in her life. She eventually became an altar server at the church, something she really loved.

When I made that decision, I didn't think it was going to miraculously make everything immediately better. All I could do

26

was to pray this would help her in some way. I remember after dropping her off on her first day of school, I went straight into the church and lit a candle, crying while I prayed to God to ease the pain of my little girl, all of my girls.

All day I couldn't stop thinking of her and praying. When I went to pick her up, I was waiting to see the reaction on her face. As a mother, I could read my children almost immediately upon looking at them.

When school let out, I spotted her in the distance and as she approached, I thought, *Here she comes! Oh my God, she's smiling! Thank you, God!* He had answered my prayer.

When she got into the car she said, "I really think I'm going to like it here."

It was one of the first times I felt myself exhale slightly. I just hugged her tightly.

Of course, things weren't always easy, and we would continue down a long road of healing, but we could only take one small step at a time and was happy that the steps were forward, at least.

I can remember looking to anything and anyone who could possibly help my children deal with the pain and anguish that they were going through. Almost immediately I reached out to a Family Grief Group for all of us. Jackie was back at school in Boston, and although I suggested she see someone to talk to professionally, she declined. I let it go because I thought she had a legitimate outlet for her grief by talking with other family members and friends she was close with. Victoria, Olivia and I began to attend a family bereavement center together on a weekly basis. We all found the "sessions" very helpful, especially Victoria, who at first didn't want to talk to anyone in a traditional therapy setting. However, she seemed to find the sessions comforting, I believe, because she was in a young group with people, mostly her own age, who had also lost their fathers. Just being around others who have gone through similar tragedies helps you feel genuinely supported even if you do not say a word.

27

This would become the place that Victoria and I would attend on a weekly basis together for a while.

I feel this group helped Olivia a bit, as well, even though she only remained in it for a short time. We went through a couple of traditional therapists until we found the right fit, someone who Olivia would be very comfortable with expressing her personal feelings as an outlet for her grief. This is why I fully believe that there are many different ways for people to get the help they need to get through their grieving process. There is not just one way to work through grief. We all need to find support in some way, however. Some journeys we cannot go alone, and sometimes we need some outside help beyond the immensely valuable love of family and friends.

I started seeing a therapist on my own pretty much immediately after Michael passed. I can clearly recall walking into my therapist's office that first time, sitting down and telling her what transpired and what my children and I were going through. Hearing myself speak those words out loud, I could not believe it was me telling that story. The phrase, *You never think it's going to happen to you* has been applied by innumerable people to countless unfortunate and tragic circumstances, but now it applied to me, and it was no longer just some throwaway cliché. Although I appreciate everything and everyone I have in my life, and I know just how precious and fleeting life is, I could not believe this was my life now, unraveling before my eyes.

When a person loses a loved one, there are levels of grieving that we go though. I believe that is a very subjective and personal experience, and is different for everyone. I do not believe there is any time limit on grief. There is an ebb and flow to grief, like the rhythm of the ocean. For me, it was just like floating in a dark, stormy sea at night not knowing when the next wave would hit. At times, especially at the beginning, waves were constantly crashing over my head, so much so that I could not catch my breath. I thought for sure I was going to drown, and I needed a life raft to survive. My daughters were in the same boat with me.

I was losing faith, I was losing hope, and I was losing my will to live. The love I have for my children was the only thing that kept me alive. I could not let them feel any more pain than they were feeling. They lost their incredible father who they loved more than anything. They could not lose their mother, too. The fight to find myself again had just begun.

Chapter 4   **MY LIFELINES**

"Don't walk in front of me, I may not follow. Don't walk behind me, I may not lead. Walk beside me, just be my friend."
~Albert Camus

They say that when you go through a catastrophic event in your life, you learn who your true friends really are, the ones who say that they are there for you and actually mean it. After Michael's death, I learned very quickly who my biggest supporters were. There was a period in those first few months, when I was completely lost in my own grief, I felt very alone and isolated, even though I was not. I don't know what I would have done if the people closest to me, my family and friends, didn't come to my rescue. These saviors didn't always necessarily have to be physically with me 24 hours a day, but by simply making their presence known, and being a phone call away, they helped me get through those dark days until I had the strength to move forward in my life.

There was an outpouring of support from the community that we lived in, as well as from family members and friends, some of whom I had not seen in years. Whether they knew Michael personally or not, their empathy during this tremendous tragedy and time of loss was a great help to my daughters and me.

Margarita Tartakovsky, M.S., an Associate Editor at *Psych Central,* wrote, "When someone is struggling, we might be at a loss for how to help. We want to reach out. But we're worried we'll do or say the wrong thing. Then we don't do anything. Or maybe we have a track record of saying or doing the wrong things. Either way, the result is the same - we keep to ourselves." Psychotherapist Lena Aburdene Derhally, MS, LPC, who worked in oncology for years noted that the best way we can support someone who's grieving is simply by being there.

I know that having someone standing by your side as you go through a difficult time is vitally important. It does not always have to be physical. In my case, the sheer magnitude of having an "army" by me mentally was the way that I made it "out of the war" alive.

'No man is an island' is the often-quoted opening line of a famous John Donne poem. It simply means that people do not thrive when isolated from others, and it is true. For me, the poem has additional meaning, as it concludes with the line; 'And therefore never send to know for whom the bell tolls; it tolls for thee.'

When you are in the throes of a traumatic experience you are not able to articulate what exactly it is that you need to get you through it. After Michael's death, I was at the mercy of what life was *bringing forth to my children and me* each day. I had some incredible friends (and still do) who told me, "I am here for you," and meant it, never leaving my side. Just having friends that would text me and ask how my daughters and I were doing meant so much. It still does to this day. There were many times when I returned home from somewhere and found that one of my friends had dropped off flowers and cards for my girls and me. These gifts were just a way of letting us know that there were people who truly cared how we were doing. The biggest way, however, were all the phone calls and the physical presence of my very good friends who would just sit by my side for hours listening to me tell the same story (mainly of my guilt and not understanding what happened to my husband) over and over again as I cried until I passed out from grief, exhaustion, or the over-consumption of wine, or sometimes both.

GETTING AWAY FROM IT ALL

When Michael passed it was just shy of our twentieth wedding anniversary. I dreaded that upcoming day more than I could possibly put into words. I wondered if I could just sleep through it. As it drew nearer, I started to feel more panicked and anxious. It was like waiting for a tsunami to hit after a massive earthquake. I needed to get away. I needed to get far away from everything that was familiar. I started to think about where I could possibly go, and then realized that my family had a friend in England. It would be so easy to just get on a plane and fly to another country. And honestly, at that moment if I could have gone to another planet it wouldn't be far enough away.

What was supposed to be an incredibly happy milestone, being married for twenty years, was now a day of profound sadness because of my broken heart and the void created by Michael's absence. I knew that it really didn't matter where I went or how far away, because I could never escape that terrible day of October 22, 2015, or the constant excruciating pain it caused me, but I got on that plane anyway and flew across the Atlantic to England.

This became a 3,000-mile lifeline, and the people I went to visit, especially Sharon and her fiancé, Tarquin, instantly became my friends forever. The last time that I saw Sharon was about 15 years prior when my two eldest daughters were small.

When I first told my mother that I wanted to go to England, my plan was to stay in a hotel close to where Sharon lived so I would have someone I could maybe get together with and show me around a country I had never been before. I wasn't looking to impose. I just wanted an escape plan.

Like any concerned mother, mine called our friend and mentioned the sudden whim I had to travel abroad on my own. Without my knowledge they created a plan together and Sharon insisted that I stay at the home she shared with her fiancé in the town, a residence that so happened to be the birthplace of William Shakespeare.

I immediately thought of a quote by Shakespeare; "Time is very slow for those who wait. Very fast for those who are scared. Very long for those who lament. Very short for those who celebrate. But for those who love, time is eternal."

Being in England was an incredibly moving experience in so many ways. I took it all in while doing my best to forget what day it was. I didn't want to know the date or the time, or anything else for that matter. I wanted to be sure I experienced all that I could. And I achieved that objective. My new friends were incredible. They made sure that every single second was filled with new experiences and lots of fun. I got to meet their families, who were some of the most gracious people I had ever met. I honestly felt like an "American Princess" by the way they treated me. The parents of my new friends and their children were all wonderful. I got to see my friend's daughter, Jessica, who I hadn't seen since she was a little girl, and now was married and expecting her first baby.

Then came "the day." Sharon decided to take me to London, where we would stay the night. The first thing she did was take me Harrods department store. For anyone who has visited Harrods in London, it is only the most luxurious shopping experience one could ever imagine. Although there wasn't a moment that I didn't have an ache in my heart, this was a place that was so full of so many different experiences that at least it kept my mind occupied, and at times mesmerized. We literally spent almost every waking hour there. There was so much to see. It was like being in a fog with so many beautiful sights, aromas and experiences. I spent so much time picking out the perfect gifts to bring back for my daughters and family. I even decided to make one of the biggest purchases that I ever made for myself.

While walking through Louis Vuitton like I was floating on a cloud, because it felt so surreal, I decided I would buy myself a small purse. It may have not been big in size, but it made up for it in price, and I instantly felt guilty for even wanting to purchase it because although I did like nice things it wasn't about the material things for me. It never was. However, it did feel pretty good being *presented* with that purse with white-gloved service. It was good as I could have hoped to feel under the circumstances, I suppose.

The entire day and night were so full that we were both exhausted, something for which I was very grateful. My hope of wanting to sleep through "that day" may not have literally happened, however it did so figuratively.

LOVE IS ETERNAL

The day after visiting Harrod's we went out to lunch and ended up at a beautiful outdoor restaurant. The sun was shining, and it was just a beautiful afternoon. I told my friend while we were eating our lunch and drinking some wine that I was so preoccupied with our shopping spree at Harrods that I didn't do much thinking about anything else, particularly dwelling on my 20th wedding anniversary. But I wasn't sure how I felt about that.

Was it wrong and selfish of me not to think of Michael all day on that day?

I knew that was exactly why I left home and came to England in the first place. I wanted to escape the tormented thoughts that this day would surely bring. In that way, I supposed my prayer had been answered.

No sooner had I expressed these feelings to Sharon, when a violinist appeared out of nowhere and started playing a song that literally made me get up and walk over to her like I was in some sort of trance.

The song was *See You Again*, and it was as if the violinist was playing just to me, and with each succeeding song I felt like Michael was trying to speak to me through the musician. It was definitely something I will never forget.

One of the other more memorable experiences that I had on my trip to England was the night that my friends took me to one of their favorite restaurants. It featured a spectacular cabinet filled with sterling silver jewelry, which my friend told me had been made by the owner and were all one-of-a-kind pieces.

Sharon suggested that I go over to the cabinet and take a look at what was inside and see if I was drawn to anything. I did, and I was instantly fixated on one particular bracelet which had an adorable charm dangling from it. I hadn't yet seen what was written on it, but I felt deep inside that I was supposed to have it in my possession. I asked to have the bracelet removed from the cabinet, and before it was opened, I took a moment to say a little prayer in my head.

Let this have meaning, I said to myself.

When the bracelet was presented to me, I saw that there was one word engraved on the charm hanging off of it. "*Love*," it said.

I truly believe that this piece of jewelry was meant specifically for me. I believe in love. I believe in true love. I never want to lose that belief. I knew what Michael and I had was true love, and just as love was in Shakespeare's time, our love is eternal.

I feel a strong sense that the universe had it all planned out and that, one day, love would find me again. It had to, since it is eternal. The scientific world speaks of matter as a substance that cannot be created or destroyed, only changed into another form. Such as it is with love. I know that Michael's love will always remain and I truly believe that he watches over the girl's and me. I feel greatly that he is one of our guardian angels guiding and protecting us somehow. Just as he did when he was alive.

When I remarried, which I write about in greater detail later in the book, I mentioned these beliefs about true love in my vows to Dennis. I am blessed beyond any shadow of a doubt to find true love in my life in two people. I will never take that for granted. It is an incredible gift. There is nothing more important to me in this life than love, and that is why I believe I was drawn to that bracelet that day. I wear it pretty much all the time. The love I believe that bracelet represents is of everyone that I love in my life, including the love of my children, which is like the air that I breathe, the love that has carried me through the darkest of days.

I came away from my trip to England with so many experiences, not the least of which are the many memories that will last a lifetime. More importantly, however, I met people who have become my friends forever. These people became important lifelines for me at a time when I needed them most.

SUPPORT SYSTEM

I consider myself extremely lucky to have so many people I call my friends. I don't use that word loosely. I believe a friend is someone that is there for you in mind and thoughts, and only wants the best for you even if you are not always together (which in adulthood is almost impossible). I have friends from high school and some from even earlier in childhood that I am thankful to say have remained my friends to this day, along with friends that I have met along life's journey, including those that I could call at 3a.m. and they would be there. I have a group of friends, Amy, Ann and Barbara, all of whom have daughters that played softball with my girls when they were small. We became a very tightly knit group of softball moms. We make it a point to always try to get together regularly for a girl's night out, which would basically be going to dinner or hanging out at one of our houses, laughing until our sides hurt. I fondly named us the "Ya-Ya's" after the movie, *The Devine Secrets of the Ya-Ya Sisterhood*. I absolutely loved that movie from the time it came out in 2002. It's about the unbreakable bond of four friends that no matter what life threw at them they remained by each other's side. The film depicted some very deep and devastating personal moments, but also triumphs that came about with great support, compassion, and understanding of the women.

The fictional drama showed how sometimes things aren't always what they seem, when judgements from others come crashing down all around you. Although the issues in the movie may be different to our own, what resonates so greatly with me is that the bonds of friendship that are forged through the ups-and-downs of life should never be taken for granted. After Michael's death, the presence of my friends didn't mean just some cozy familiarity, but one of great importance and survival. Unfortunately, what was mostly laughing until our sides hurt quickly turned into deep emotional trauma and wiping the tears of devastation from my face. In life, we never lose friends. We only learn who the true ones are.

Someone once said to me that the second year of grief is more difficult than the first year because as time goes on there may be a waning of what is called "our support and/or lifelines." As a result, it is natural to feel more isolated and alone after that first year, but I did not have this experience exactly. I really only began to feel a "division of support" after I met Dennis.

For some people it seemed acceptable for me to be grieving alone while struggling to cope with the hand that life had dealt my family. However, there seemed to be a shift in perspective among some in my support group the moment I met someone. I recall that after Michael's death, I basically made social media my journal, in some way. I would post photos and write things I was feeling on that particular day. I was devastated and was falling lower and lower into the darkest depths of my own mind. I believe that's when God decided he needed to throw me another lifeline. That lifeline's name was Dennis. Looking back, I remember there was a person frequently posting inspirational quotes and verses to me. Many were very deeply emotional. Some were about Romeo and Juliet, interestingly enough. We are all familiar with that story of eternal love and double suicide. At the time, I wasn't exactly sure why someone would think it was a good idea to post something like that to a recent widow whose husband had committed suicide, but at the time I found the posts to be sweet and thoughtful. Then later, when Dennis entered my life, I remember after some people had seen us together, they would react negatively. A few people went so far as to unfriend me on social media. Interestingly enough, one happened to be the person who would quote Romeo and Juliet. I only found out about this cyber slight much later because, honestly, this person wasn't a very significant person in my life. This was when I started to feel a general "shift in the air," a change in attitude toward the judgmental side by some.

I heard through the grapevine that some people couldn't believe that I actually was seeing someone. I began to receive

37

negative, anonymous messages and mail about me being with another man. Some would have comments such as, "If you loved Michael so much how could you be with someone else *so fast*?" I even had someone else go so far as to say to me that they initially blamed me for Michael's death. They said I should have "seen the signs" and saved him. It was amazing that people could pass judgement on something about which they had absolutely no idea.

There were so many cruel, ignorant and misinformed comments going around which I found incredibly disturbing. These people did not know what I was feeling. From the day Michael died, I continued to exist as if he was still there, feeling each passing day, then weeks, and months. I felt every painful second. I was with him for twenty-three years, so every single moment without him was like a knife in my heart, like the one that Juliet plunged into herself. God's plan was not to make my children orphans and make my story end like *Romeo and Juliet*.

This took its toll on me emotionally. My true friends and those who just wanted to see me smile again were still there for me to help get me through this painful time when I was beginning to rebuild my life. The guilt that I felt on so many levels was inescapable, and I did not need anyone else to make me feel worse than I did about it. It was always with me, like a shadow of my previous life, which had materially changed but continued to silently walk beside me.

How could I have loved someone so much and then be able to have a connection like that with another man? How could that be possible? I would ask myself these questions just trying to make sense of it in my own mind.

I didn't know it at the time, but I strongly felt that God's plan included Dennis coming into my life when he did. Dennis and I both feel that we were brought together. This sense is so profound for me I feel that Michael could have even had a hand in it. He would never want to see me continuing down the path I was headed before Dennis came into my life. Michael would have never wanted me to live my life alone. Yet even though being with Dennis felt "right," I couldn't completely escape the guilt and the divergent flood of emotions that came with having him in my life. If my own struggles over this weren't enough, these anonymously sent letters of judgement and condemnation were shocking and hurtful. I was confused enough, and I couldn't understand the mindset of these people.

How could they possibly fathom my tumultuous pain and the horrific ordeal my children and I were living? The answer is they couldn't, because if they did, they wouldn't be trying to create any further pain and suffering in our lives.

I kept thinking to myself that I didn't leave Michael. This wasn't a divorce or a separation. Michael was gone. He died and he wasn't coming back. Why was I being treated as if I had some type of choice?

I have tried to eliminate these people from my life in the past few years. Anyone that was causing negativity in any way was someone I did not need to have around me. This was not helping my children and me move forward. It was hindering our growth when all I wanted for us was to grow and keep getting better.

I have always tried not to be a judgmental person in my life, but looking back, in complete honestly, I too have probably looked at the situations others were going through and thought, *I know exactly what I would do if I was them,* or say, *Wow, I can't believe they could do this or that.* However, I look at things differently now. Now I will look at such things and think, *I don't know what I would do because I haven't been in that situation.* And if I were in a similar situation, I would try to be empathetic, realizing that no matter how similar a situation is, it is not the SAME situation, so you cannot fully know what it's like for someone else. Never presume to know.

One time, while at lunch with my friend Amy, we were joking and laughing when she suddenly looked me in the eye, most empathetically and said, "I never thought I would see you like this again. Honestly, I didn't think you were going to make it through this."

I looked back at her, with tears welling up in both of our eyes, and I said, "I didn't either."

It sounds dramatic, but there was a time I really felt I would not survive. Amy knew because she saw the everyday struggle I went through and the false smile I wore like a mask. It's easy to throw stones and make comments that are hurtful to others, but I think as a society we should start to be more caring and compassionate towards others, especially to those who are going through a traumatic situation.

Sometimes people internalize situations and make them more about themselves rather than about those who are in the midst of it all, the ones "on the front lines" trying to learn how to live each day again and become whole. Trying to just survive can be a big enough challenge. So, if someone you know and care about is suffering in some way, be a lifeline, not an anchor.

Chapter 5   **FAITH TESTED**

"For I will walk by faith even when I cannot see." ~2
Corinthians 5:7

In a time of loss, many people are comforted by their
religious beliefs, while others who are struggling to make sense
of a death begin to question their faith. I, surprisingly, found
myself to be in the latter category. Eventually I came to the
conclusion that the tragedy which befell my family was a test of
my spirituality.

I have always considered myself a woman of strong faith.
I never believed in coincidences. I always felt that everything
happens for a reason, and when things are supposed to happen to
you, they happen. Fate and destiny were things I had never
questioned before. Then Michael died. I had a very hard time
reconciling that harsh fact with what I believed as a Catholic, or
what I was supposed to believe.

You often hear the biblical anecdote, "those who believe
need not grieve." This paraphrase is taken from 1 Thessalonians
4:13 in which Paul provides helpful instruction to grief-stricken
Christians with these words: "We do not want you to be
uninformed, brothers, about those who are asleep, that you may
not grieve as others do who have no hope."

The text does not say that we shouldn't grieve, just that
we should grieve differently than those who have no hope. The
Bible does not dismiss or minimize grief, and Jesus himself wept
at the death of his friend Lazarus. Jesus not only lost his good
friend Lazarus to death, he also lost his dear friend and cousin,
John the Baptist. Yet, as I thought about losing Michael, I
realized that I felt no comfort. This made me wonder if I was a
true believer, or if I ever really believed. This was very
disheartening for me, having always been a practicing Catholic,
going to church and abiding the sacraments and teachings of the
Church. Suddenly a very personal, spiritual debate was waging
within me over the issues of faith and God. If I was still feeling

the full pain of grief many months after Michael's death, I wondered how could I believe in God?

I was angry that my husband, a devoted father of our three daughters, my best friend, had been taken from me. It wasn't supposed to happen. He was too young. We were the perfect family. What reason could God have to take all that away from us? I didn't understand God's plan. I was always taught to trust in God because there is always a plan. What would the plan be for this? For the suffering of my daughters and me and countless others who loved him? As time passed, I became angrier, not less.

There were many times that I would question God's plan, and why He would take so many innocent lives that just seemed to begin to live. However, I always felt that when a person's life ended it was because their life here on this earthly plane was complete. I always believed that we are put on this earth to not only learn something ourselves but to also be part of others' life lessons and journeys. When that lesson is complete God takes them *home*. Others are left behind to suffer the loss. There has to be some reason for *this*? It is often very difficult to fathom all the suffering. I want to believe that we become stronger in the strife in our fight to survive the pain. Is it within this pain that we realize the potential of our own lives; the potential of living, of loving, of kindness, empathy, forgiveness, compassion, or whatever has hindered us from our true meaning of our own lives? Maybe our lessons are built in the pain somehow. In order to make sense in my own mind, it has to be.

I did a lot of reading on the subject, much soul-searching, and hours of counseling before I came to realize that grieving a loss, for any length of time, does not mean you have lost your faith. Grief is a feeling of separation from someone you love and coming to terms with the reality that you will not be with that person anymore. I do believe that on some plane, at least, it gets easier with time, but the pain never goes away.

At the height of my own grief, when the pain was at its worst, I had no idea what faith meant anymore. I had always maintained faith in my marriage, in my family, and in my life even during the most trying times, an unwavering belief that things would somehow take my family and me down the right path, the course that our lives were predestined to take. This was the belief that I tried to instill in my children, as well. When our worlds suddenly came crashing down, I wasn't certain what I believed in anymore. I certainly didn't believe in myself or what I had always believed to be true in the past. I started questioning everything, and I know that this doubt was what caused the darkness to infiltrate my life and overtake everything. Not willingly, or even knowingly, the profound depth of despair in which I was languishing made it easy for me to question the basis of all the things I stood for, and I just became lost in the darkness of my despair.

Looking back now, I not only recognized how terrified I was at the time, but also how numb I had become to everything else. I believe in the dual existence of both good and evil in life, and that when you are at your lowest you are most vulnerable to evil, and susceptible to the darkness that dwells within all of us. People may have different personal and spiritual beliefs, but I feel that when you are at your weakest, this is when the threat is greatest that you will fall to your lowest form. That was what happened to me. I saw my children struggle with their faith and shaken to their most raw vulnerable cores at times and I felt so helpless because no matter what I did I could not take away their pain. I could only show them that I was there for them.

Thankfully, we had our family and close friends who didn't believe the false smiles and brave masks that we tried to put on for them. We were lucky to have people that truly loved and kept in contact with us to see how we were doing.

Many of my good friends would make it a point to text or call me each day to check in on me. They seemed to be able to decipher my mood from my texts. They made a point of stopping over to make sure things were okay. Of course, things weren't always okay, but they were always there to help me through the pain. For that. and for them, I will always be eternally grateful.

LOSING THE ESSENCE OF YOURSELF

I draw back to a memory I have of the time I went out for a job interview at a large business development staffing firm. I was led into a large conference room, and the man interviewing me asked me to sit down at a table with about twenty empty chairs, including one on either end. Now, I could have sat in any one of those chairs, and most people would have chosen a chair somewhere in the middle, yet I walked all the way to the head of the table in stiletto heels and my best career-driven, goal-oriented pantsuit and sat down. I remember just after sitting thinking, *"Oh my God, what the heck did I just do?"* I remained calm (at least on the outside), and when my interviewer said, "I find it interesting that you chose the head of the table to sit." I replied, "Well, I know that the person you are looking to fill this position is someone who isn't afraid to take charge, and needs to be in control. I feel that's who I am and that's who you want."

I was hired. They liked me for being the strong person in control, who knew exactly what needed to be done and wouldn't stop until the job was done.

On October 22, 2015 that strong woman became a distant memory, and for a long time I went through each succeeding day replaying what happened on that fateful day over and over in my mind. And then I began to blame myself.

My 95-year old grandmother had died just days before Michael took his own life, and I was so caught up in the sorrow over losing of one of the strongest women and one of the biggest influences in my life that I started to wonder if it had distracted me from being available to Michael, sufficient enough so that I could not perceive what he was going through at that time, and as a result not able to help him. Could things have turned out differently for Michael if I wasn't mourning my grandmother and simultaneously trying to make sense of what was happening with him? Had I missed any of the signs that he may have given that he was going to end his life in the next few days?

I don't believe that to be true today, but at that time, I was battling those thoughts and I was sure I had let my husband down. Michael and I had always been keenly in tune with each other's thoughts and feelings, and when something wasn't making sense, or when what he was telling me didn't make sense, I did EVERYTHING I could to help him. This time, however, the universe, or God, had other plans.

While I do not think I could have changed the way things turned out, for a very long time I was haunted by what I didn't know and what I didn't do. I suppose these are thoughts that will never completely go away. The mystery of it will always remain.

At the end, his conversations with everyone but me were forced, and I could see that Michael was not himself. He did not want to speak to anyone. He didn't answer his phone.

"Michael, all your friends are calling and texting you to see how you are doing," I told him. "You have to call them or text them back!"

"Janine, they don't care." He sounded agitated. "They are just calling to see when I am going back to work, or out of some sense of obligation."

I didn't understand. "What do you mean? These are your friends that have been friends with you for years. They care about you. They aren't calling you out of obligation."

No matter how much I tried to reason with him, he didn't seem to change what he was thinking. The problem was I had no idea where these thoughts were coming from, but never for a minute did I believe that there was something happening to his mental state. Not until the very end. I just could not understand why he was thinking these things.

Was there really something happening to him that was making him think this way?

I couldn't find a reason for it.

He had some pretty incredible friends. People he had been

close with for many years, and some who he had become closer with in recent years and who I became friends with, as well. We were all a big part of each other's lives, some twenty years and more, some less but certainly not less important to our lives. There was no way that they would have anything but love and support for him.

Michael had been out of work at that time because of a knee injury, and perhaps that had been a factor. He always had problems with his knees, ever since I'd known him. He had multiple knee surgeries on both his knees, and even had a knee replacement at the age of forty because the pain had gotten so bad. It was such a shame because he was a very fit and active man, which was pretty much the reason for all of the knee injuries and issues. He was always in the gym lifting weights and loved being outside throwing the ball around with our girls. He'd frequently be outside shooting baskets with his friends and playing pickup games until he just couldn't do it anymore because his knees would not allow it. It was very discouraging for him, and the replacement surgery unfortunately didn't help change anything. His mobility would never be the same. But he never complained, so I couldn't imagine that his knees were causing this sudden despondency and distrust of everyone. But it had to be something. He just was not close to being the Michael that I knew.

No matter how hard I tried, there was nothing I could do to keep things from spiraling downward. I even tried to employ what I believed in most; my faith in God and my faith in prayer. My trust that good prevailed over evil.

After that terrible day in October, I asked myself, "What do you believe in?"

There was no easy answer to that question, and it would take me some time before I could regain a sense of myself and return to the person I was before. What I came to realize was that the most important thing was finding some way to bring my daughters, who relied on me so much, through the worst storms of their lives. When we finally did emerge from the storm later, we were not the same as we were before. However, it proves that we all have the ability to rise up from the deepest depths of despair.

The skies would only begin to clear when I came to understand that the path I was on without faith and hope was a very dark and dangerous one. I would rather remain on a brightly lit path with my faith and hope, being guided forward, rather than trapped in the darkness without hope and nothing in which to believe.

It is certainly not easy, but by taking small steps, even when it may be hard to breathe at times, you will ultimately find your way out of it with something called faith, hope and the love of others, and in the end the love for yourself.

Chapter 6   **CHANGES**

"God grant me the Serenity to accept the things I cannot change, Courage to accept the things I can and Wisdom to know the difference."

Michael's death and his absence from my life and the lives of our three daughters brought very profound changes to all of us, and we continue to feel the effects today, as I'm sure we always will to some extent. As a matter of survival and preservation, we had to fight to figure out a new way to remain a supportive and strong family while simultaneously feeling the immense void without this amazing man, husband, and father, in our lives.

Neurologists have recently discovered that even when parts of the brain have been damaged, destroyed or even missing, the remaining parts can learn how to take over the functions that were lost. Like the mysterious and complex anatomy of the human brain the human will is just as resilient and regenerative.

To say that things "changed" is the biggest understatement one can utter. People often change jobs, schools, homes and many other things. People and lives do naturally progress and change. Although all of the above would be the case for my girls and me, it was the sum of all these changes at once that was so devastating. We were stripped of everything that we knew, and we were forced to change the only world we had ever known. It was like living in an alternate universe. We had absolutely no idea what this new life would be like, even though we were already living it. What we had before Michael died was everything that anyone could want in this life, at least everything that *we wanted*. We were happy, content, and we had a family that was whole. What we had now was broken and devastated. I remember thinking that we would never be able to do things as a complete family unit again. We wouldn't be able to take drives to Beavertail in Jamestown, our family spot, by the big rock. The place where we used to fly kites and sit on the rocks by the ocean and picnic together. We wouldn't be able to take our annual family trip to Salem, Massachusetts at Halloween time, which we had done since the girls were small. Sadly, that was the last family trip we took together, just two weeks before Michael passed. I wouldn't be able to sit in the yard and watch the four of them throw the softball around while laughing and teasing each other while I smiled to myself knowing what a blessing this was.

Some months after Michael passed, I was visiting my mother when I became lost in my own thoughts and decided to go for walk outside to get some air. It was early spring. The trees were full of lush green leaves and the bushes were all overgrown, but there was a slight chill in the air and a sweet fragrance that drew me toward the scent. I felt compelled to walk through the back fence and into the woods in the back of my mother's house where we had lived for a few years. I stopped beside the blossoming lilac tree that we had uprooted and took with us each time we moved to a new house. Lilacs were my favorite, and Michael was determined to get that lilac tree to bloom for me. It hadn't bloomed at our previous house, but he was determined that one day this tree would bloom for me. Ironically, they began to bloom most abundantly the year after he passed.

Under the brush and weeds behind my mother's house I saw an old net and the softball batting tee that Michael and the girls once used for batting practice. As I stood there, I felt a soft breeze blow through my hair. It was like a breath being given to me, as I almost felt I was losing a bit of mine. In my mind's eye I saw Michael sitting on an empty bucket tossing softballs to Jackie to hit into the net while the other girls were running all around playing in the yard. I could hear the sound of the bat hitting the ball and see them playing catch in the yard. Their voices and laughter whispered softly in my ear.

"Ready, girls?"

It was a scene that played out almost every evening in the spring when the girls were little.

"Jackie, fill the bucket of balls and get your glove. Come on, Victoria. Olivia, you too."

"Do I have to, Dad?"

"Yes, you do."

So many people come home after a long day of work and just want to unwind watching TV or go out with friends to grab a beer. Michael's way to unwind and relax was to spend time with his family.

"You should have caught that!" one of the girls would yell to another and an argument would sometimes ensue. But Michael had a way of getting them to play nice together, and ultimately it was the laughter that would consume them all. It was something special to see. I knew it then.

Besides the softballs, I can still hear Michael tossing around Italian-American slang words such as *"Madonn'!"* and *"Momma mia!"* Or the expressions, "You're giving me *agita!"*(heartburn), and "What a *sfacimm!"* He spoke these words with emphasis in a funny way if one of the girls were being fresh when they were small. We still smile remembering some of the words he used most often. My daughters, especially Olivia, will sometimes say some of them exactly the way he used to, particularly, *"Madonna mi!"*

Michael coached many of their youth teams. He loved every minute of it and the girls loved having him as a coach. The whole team did. He was fair and didn't just play his daughter's out of favoritism. He played everyone equally and fairly, and you can determine that because the parents all loved him as well. He was very athletic and knew the game well. All the girls would say they learned a lot from his coaching and there was always laugher and fun on the field.

When the girls got to high school and travel ball started, Michael absolutely hated it if he had to miss any of their games. We made it a point that even if one of us was not able to make it to a game due to work responsibilities, the other would provide play-by-play coverage of the action via texting. And we did. Michael didn't have to miss a minute of how the girls and their teams were doing. Some of my texts were inadvertently funny.

ACCEPTING THINGS THAT CANNOT BE CHANGED

One of the hardest things was not having any explanation, not being able to rationalize what went so wrong so quickly. There was just a permanent hole in our hearts. Even though we had one another, this was a personal, internal battle that each of us needed to go through alone. The struggle of taking the first steps forward in this completely different life proved to be some of the most difficult, and at times most traumatic, experiences for each of us.

For me, believing that there are no coincidences in life means that there is just a path upon which we travel that takes us to a higher place of being. One minute we can seemingly feel like the world is "as it should be" then in the next moment life as we know it can be obliterated without cause, reason, or explanation. We can spend the rest of our lives questioning, blaming others and ourselves, hating, doubting everything (and that is very easy to do) or we can be open to when we see and feel some flicker of a light that I call HOPE, and try to understand that this is our own personal journey. This is an experience that is wonderful but at times difficult and painful.

When one is stuck in the darkness of pain and heartache and it seems as if there is no way out, sometimes a glimmer of light will appear and we need to not question why. Instead, we must follow this light as our beacon out of the darkness. I would call this faith, and no one can walk this path of life for us. We must walk in our own shoes and follow the signs that will deliver us.

This was the most difficult part for me to accept because of my children. I wanted to be able to walk the path of pain for them and shield them from the hurt in every way, but I couldn't. I could support and guide my daughters, but ultimately, they had to complete their own journey in their own way, just as I had to do. It wasn't always easy, but we had faith that we would ultimately find the peace in our hearts that we desperately needed.

I think back to a moment a few years prior to Michaels passing. We were in Salem, MA, for our annual, October, day trip. The streets are always lined with arts and crafts, food and festivities. I always liked to look at the different vendors' spaces that would be set up. They would be selling an array of things from candles, clothing and jewelry to hot chocolate and popcorn and everything in between. It was then that I remember a small silver medallion catching my eye. It was a symbol of the lotus flower with its meaning enclosed on an insert within the box. It mentioned how the lotus flower grows through muddy waters towards the light where it then emerges perfectly clean and beautiful. Although it grows through adverse situations, it symbolizes purity and harmony. I instantly knew this was something I wanted to purchase. It was something I would wear almost daily from that day forward. I felt a connection to the meaning of the lotus flower which holds such power because of its ability to inspire *hope* to those struggling to grow through everyday life. I just didn't realize how much meaning it would hold for me until the days when I would find myself struggling to find my way back into the light.

I remember the day I became a widow and a single parent. Those things may have happened the instant Michael passed, but for me it really rang true when I was confronted with a simple form that I had to fill out and provide my personal information. It was sometime after the funeral, as I was trying to find ways to come to terms with my grief, I was challenged with a question about my marital status. I had to check a previously unfamiliar box, the last box, beyond the Single, Married, and Divorced boxes – the box for Widowed.

I was at my doctor's office at the time, and I began to cry like a baby. That's when it hit me. I went from having everything figured out in my mind to not even knowing who I was anymore.

Trauma permanently changes us. One thing I have learned about trauma and that is that there is no such thing as "getting over it." We must go through the stages of grief and somehow learn to accept the loss, which is a major feat. At least it was in my experience. With the traumatic loss of a loved one there is also a traumatic loss of ourselves, the people we knew ourselves to be. There was no going back to the "old me" because that person no longer existed.

I continue to find this to be one of the most difficult hurdles to overcome, one that I work hard to deal with during my therapy sessions. I always seemed to define myself by the role or title I had in life. I was a wife, a mother, and a teacher for a time. In more recent years, when working in the business world, I *was* whatever my title stated. I seemed to identify with that title, I think mainly because I had a very clear sense of myself. When someone asked, "What do you do?" I immediately had an answer. It seems that as a society we identify ourselves and each other from a laundry list of questions that define who we are by our occupation, titles, where we live, what we drive instead of by what should be the only criteria worth judging ourselves by; *are we happy? Are we content?*

After Michael passed, I ceased working outside the home, the reason being that I needed to be there for my children, whose lives were turned upside down. It was sheer pain and confusion, especially my youngest, Olivia, who was really outwardly struggling to make it through each day.

I also dropped out of the workforce temporarily because I couldn't think straight, and I would not have been able to concentrate on any professional duties, or trying to solve the problems of other people in a business setting. I had very abruptly been stripped of the clear sense of my identity that I had, and as a result I became a stranger to myself. I no longer felt able to define myself by any role or title. Although I was still a mother, a title for which I will forever hold the utmost regard, who I was beyond that role was uncertain at best. It was a dark, frightening world at that time. Everything instantly changed and I went from wife and mother with a career, working in a very fast-paced business environment in the city and enjoying the responsibility and respect it brought me, to a widow and a single parent without a clue as to how this happened or what to do next. I would spend the next few years struggling to figure this out, both in and out of my regular therapy sessions.

At some point we must be able to come to a 'new normal,' and with that there emerges a new person out of that trauma. The goal is to be able to heal in order to find a new way to discover strength and joy within this new person you are becoming. This is all part of an internal struggle. It's a process, and a very personal one. You are the only one that can hold yourself up and remain standing. However, it is important to know that it is ok to ask for help. We can't always do it alone. I know because I tried for a long time to shoulder the entire burden by myself and tackle all of the responsibilities so my children wouldn't have to do it. It was inevitable that I would reach a breaking point. Ultimately, others can help you up, but only you can find a way to keep yourself moving forward one step at a time and hopefully transform into a person that, although changed, is able to pick up each broken piece, put them together and wear them like a badge of courage.

ESCAPING CHRISTMAS

We were coming up on Christmas, always my favorite time of the year, but I couldn't bear to even think of seeing a tree, hearing a Christmas carol, or anything else associated with the holiday. It was just two months after Michael had passed. I could imagine the enormous void that was going to be felt by my children and me, and there was absolutely no way I was going to let that happen. We needed to get out of the familiar. I wanted out and I didn't want to come back until we were into a new year, so I went to the travel agent and I booked my girls, my sister and me on a trip to the Dominican Republic. Of course, I couldn't have done any of this by myself. I needed the support of my family. I realized that no matter where we went, we wouldn't be able to escape the pain, but staying back home would be even worse. Before we even left, I got a jolt back to reality that I did not expect.

When I took the girls to get their passports, the woman

56

helping us informed me that their father's consent was required for them to leave the country because they were under the age of 18.

It would not be the only time I felt such a "sucker punch," but I did not see the magnitude of this one coming and it stung me. I knew that I would need a death certificate that day, which I had at-the-ready, and I handed her a copy robotically without saying anything. The woman gasped, and then began to do something that still shocks me every time other people do the same thing. She began to ask me questions, highly personal and difficult questions, including how Michael had died and how old he was. Asking these questions to me was bad enough but asking them in front of my children was that much worse.

Not knowing how to respond to this woman, I looked at her and calmly said, "I would rather not talk about it."

She respected my feelings, and didn't say anything more, which is not always the case. It infuriates me that people would be so intrusive to ask questions like that and then continue to try to pry even when it is clear that the person is not comfortable talking with them about a recent death of a loved one. I understand that people are curious, but they just don't always know how painful it is to talk about such a thing with a complete stranger. I don't think I have ever done this to someone I didn't know, but after experiencing it myself, it's definitely something I would never do to another person. When you become aware of another person's grief, it would be much more considerate and compassionate to simply offer your condolences and leave it at that. If the person who lost a loved one then wants to discuss the situation, that it is up to them.

It was extremely emotional at the beginning, and it was especially difficult because of the manner in which Michael passed. It always feels like such a violation of my privacy to even be asked that question because the answer would always require an explanation, one that I certainly wouldn't want to give to people I barely know. There was guilt and shame, which we will discuss in more detail later, which no one would understand unless they had gone through something like that themselves. The incredulous looks and the judgmental stares are typically not something you get when you tell people your husband passed away from an illness or an accident.

We were all looking forward to getting out of the state and going somewhere we would hopefully not see anything resembling a "traditional Christmas." I wanted to get out of Rhode Island so badly that I felt like I was on auto pilot. I was disconnected from my body. While we were in line at the airport, someone from TSA asked the crowd if anyone was going to St. Maarten. I raised my hand, and as the TSA employee started to come over to us my sister immediately grabbed my hand and pulled it down. "We're not going to St. Maarten," she said. "We're going to the Dominican!"

We laughed about it afterward, but it was clearly an indication that my mind was not exactly functioning at 100% and I needed to get away from it all for a while.

The resort was absolutely breathtaking and the only sign of Christmas was a large decorated tree near the middle of the resort. Still, it was nothing like it would have been at home. All I wanted out of this little getaway was to see my girls smiling again. That's something that hasn't changed to this day. Whenever I hear them laughing it breathes life into my soul. They were the only thing keeping me alive. Every day, I tried to keep them occupied with different activities. We went parasailing, snorkeling, and we swam with the Dolphins, which I found to be totally exhilarating and somewhat therapeutic. It was very calming just being around them. That was something I desperately needed. I had to find a way to take a breath without it feeling excruciating. I needed to sleep through the night without being tormented by nightmares and shocked to wakefulness by the circumstances of a new life to which I still had not been able to adjust. I was praying for even the slightest feelings of acceptance and recovery for us all during this trip and I specifically remember authorizing my daughters to sign for whatever they wanted at the swim-up bars and cafés each day.

Obviously, they were only getting sodas or some type of frozen virgin cocktail. At one point one of the waiters asked my sister and me where "the little one was." He was talking about Olivia.

I said, "She's at the bar."

"Again?" he asked.

This made us laugh, and it felt really good. Turning around then, I saw Olivia at the bottom of a coconut tree which a man was climbing to get another coconut for her virgin Pina colada, probably her fourth of the day. It was kind of comical, though probably not for the guy climbing the coconut tree every half hour. He had probably been looking to hide from my little 11-year-old by that point, but I didn't care. Whatever made her smile and allowed her to focus, even if only temporary, on something fun and not dwell on the devastating loss of her father was the only thing I cared about. I, on the other hand, had an agreement with a specific waiter, who I asked to do only one thing for me each day. If he was to ever see me without a cocktail at any given time, he was to bring me one ASAP. He may have been obliged because I always tipped well, but I only wanted to be sure I removed myself as far from my reality as I could, which I would soon learn was not so easy to do. Trying to escape truth, however, only makes it worse.

We had a bit of an adventure on the day we went on a parasailing/snorkeling excursion. As my girls were floating atop the surface of the beautiful azure waters of the Caribbean, surrounded by fish of every imaginable color, my sister and I stayed on the boat and watched them, taking it all in. About an hour later, dance music suddenly came on and they started to pass out drinks.

What the heck had I done?

That's when I realized that I had booked us on a Booze Cruise. My girls all laughed at me when they found out. Olivia, said, "Mommy! You took us on a Booze Cruise?"

"No! I absolutely did not!" However, I remember later going through the resort pamphlet frantically hoping that I wasn't so *out of it* that I actually had mistakenly done what even Olivia believed. Thank God, nowhere was there any mention of a Booze Cruise (sigh of relief).

We actually all had a great time. Everyone was dancing, including the girls, my sister and me. It was part of a short-lived escape from reality spent lying by the pool and by the ocean, as well as doing some sort of activity each day. However, in the end, it didn't change anything for me. The fact was that as soon as the vacation was over, I was without Michael, and that I still had to find a way to make a life for my daughters without their father.

I didn't know what I was going to do. The reality was frightening.

Immediately upon leaving the Dominican, we went to visit family members in Florida, where we spent the New Year before returning home. The same deep, penetrating agony was waiting there for me, and it was obvious that the only way I was going to have any chance of a healthy and happy life for me and the girls was to move. As big of a decision as this was, and as much effort as such an undertaking would require, it had to be done. I started the process right away and began looking at houses.

A SCARY STEP FORWARD

Four months after Michael passed, I felt I needed to begin looking for a new home for my girls and me. Michael and I had been in the process of looking for a new home before he died, and I felt I needed to continue to do so even though I had never done anything this big on my own before. We needed a comfortable, stable environment, a place to call home where we could embark on a new normal way of life.

I was driving with my father one day and we were looking at a couple of houses of interest while a feeling of intense despair and isolation suddenly came over me. I thought I was going to be sick. Somehow, I managed to hold back tears long enough to get back to my mother's house. I could not hide my anguish, however, and my dad asked if I was okay. I nodded hopelessly and went up to my room where I put my head into my hands and sobbed uncontrollably. This sense of hopelessness and despair became a common occurrence for a very long time after.

After a month, and not finding anything to my liking, I finally happened upon a cute Colonial that I was drawn to instantly. I was driving around with my sister when we spotted the FOR SALE sign in the yard. There was a little section of a white picket fence and the ample yard was neatly landscaped. The house was set far back from the road and it had a long driveway. It had recently snowed so the yard was covered in white. It was beautiful. There didn't seem to be anyone living there as my sister got out of the car to look around. She went to the back gate and opened it, and a moment later she came back with sheer excitement on her face.

"Come and see this!" she practically sang. "There's a built-in pool and a *huge* fenced in yard." My sister knew I would love it and she was right. This was all the persuading I needed. I called a friend whose husband was a realtor. I'd trusted him to help me buy and sell some of my properties in the past. The day I talked to him he said he could get me in to see the house within the hour.

The path to my future and a new life for my girls and me was slowly being revealed to me and I was determined to keep following it.

When I looked at the house, I thought, *If I ever buy this house, I will add to it something that I have dreamt of since I was a little girl, that being a farmer's porch complete with a chair swing.*

The porch swing would be the first Christmas gift that Dennis bought me. I remember opening it up and a flood of emotions overwhelming me to the point I started sobbing because he had just given to me a piece of what I had always envisioned as representative of a perfect sense of happiness and calm. Something he, himself, would also prove to be in my life.

This would end up being part of a new reality for me, as this has since become the house that Dennis and I and the girls call home today. I 100% feel I was led to this house by a higher power. I know that if Michael could have brought me here himself, he would have.

Maybe in some way he did.

Incredibly, I purchased my first home on my own. Though I knew it was the right thing, my emotions were all over the place, and seemed to change by the hour. I was on my way, anyway, to whatever lay ahead.

Chapter 7   **NUMBING THE PAIN**

"We cannot selectively numb emotions, when we numb the painful emotions, we also numb the positive emotions." ~ Brené Brown

They say things get worse before they get better. I didn't believe they could get any worse, so maybe that's why I thought numbing myself with alcohol would not hurt me, only dull the pain a little.

I was very wrong about that.

It made a horrible situation much worse, which only brought me to my breaking point that much sooner. It didn't help alleviate any of the burden, it only added to my anxiety and depression and ability to cope with everything.

At first, I justified my excessive consumption of alcohol. I deserved it. It was only a bottle of wine.

During the day, I did my best to walk through the days like a normal person that could handle things while feeling like I had a knife lodged in my heart. I was barely able to breathe but I did a good job of seeming "OK." When it came to my girls, however, I felt I didn't falter. I would fight with everything in my being to take care of them, whatever I had to do.

At night, I would shut the door and put on music, listening to "our songs" as I looked at photographs and read through old texts and letters and listen to old voicemail messages from Michael. I would even read through the autopsy report, as well as the police reports, including all of the accounts of the police officers who were there that day. As I picked through these files, I would be holding Michael's clothes, including the blood-stained shirt and pants he was wearing when he died. I immersed myself in what happened to him, what happened to us, and I blamed everyone and everything.

One bottle of wine became two bottles, and it became easier to drink as well as lie to myself. I was really just running away from my problem, and running away from reality. But I would not accept that there was no way that someone couldn't have saved him, even if that someone was me.

In life, people seem to find one way or another to cope with the tragedies and pain that life can sometimes throw at us. Some may turn to alcohol, some turn to drugs, while still others find their comfort in the overindulgence of food. Some will chase after unhealthy relationships. Some may throw themselves into their work or projects so that they can try to keep their minds busy with constant stimulation. In the beginning, and for quite a while afterward, my mind was excruciatingly stimulated enough in the "real world" 24 hours a day. Every day, I took on everything that involved my children, including all that was happening in our life in this alternate universe we were now living in. My only concern was making sure they were okay. I couldn't stand to see them in pain, and I came to realize how much they couldn't stand to see me in pain, which was why I tried to hide it, dull it, anyway possible.

Each night it was the same routine. I would sit by the fire pit in the backyard of our new beautiful home alone with a drink in my hand to try to blunt the pain of what felt like my soul ripping into pieces as I stared blankly around the darkness trying to figure out where this life was going to take us. By doing this, I thought I was concealing much, if not all of my pain from my children. Little did I know that they easily saw through this charade, even my youngest, and it bothered them greatly. My behavior was only adding to their worry, the exact opposite of what my intentions had been.

Many nights, one of my very good friends would come and sit with me and talk with me and cry with me while listening to the same recollections over and over again. The recounting of the days and excruciating moments of *that day* over and over again. The accounts of a broken shell of a woman who had absolutely no idea where her life was going, but my friends didn't seem to mind. They just wanted to be there for me, and they were. Occasionally my daughters would come out and sit with me. I would talk to them and try to help them sort through all the feelings of grief and abandonment with which they were grappling. Sometimes they would talk, sometimes they would just sit there and listen to me. We are an extremely strong family unit, and if one of us was down we would rally together and lift each other up. This became much harder to do now that we were all sitting in the same life raft trying our best to stay afloat while the waves continually crashed over us. We were all in so much pain, and it was hard to contemplate that there would come a day when we wouldn't feel so incredibly devastated, a day when we wouldn't cry ourselves to sleep at night or lay awake wondering what happened to our perfectly seamless life.

PILGRIMAGE AND PRAYER

My self-numbing didn't always involve drinking, which was definitely more than I had ever done in my life. In my *previous life* I wasn't running away from anything. I was able to enjoy having a glass of wine or two without the overwhelming sadness I was experiencing after losing Michael.

As a practicing Catholic, I took my children to church every Sunday. After Michael died, however, I couldn't even walk into church without crying. The ringing bells would instantly transport my mind to so many places. Places where I was feeling so many different emotions. The bells from when I was little at my grandmother's house, the bells of growing up and running into church, the bells from my wedding day, and the bells from Michael's funeral, all merged in my mind. I wanted to be able to enter the church without feeling a crushing, overwhelming sadness. I wanted to once again find the comfort there that I once did. But I could not.

The only time I went to church, alone or with my children, was to light a candle and say a prayer. I would pray so hard for peace for my daughters and for me. I had to find a way to feel something again. Something other than numbness and pain. It wouldn't be until I went to Italy with my mother the year after Michael passed that I would be able to find the peace in the churches that I so longed to find. A visit to the Vatican in Rome and praying each day in different chapels began to breathe life back into my wearied soul. We went to Europe basically on a kind of pilgrimage. Our group would walk in the same places and pray in the same chapels that St. Francis of Assisi, the patron saint of Italy and the patron saint of animals, had been known to walk and pray during the 1200's.

We went with a small group of people who we did not know, including a well-known local medium who organized the trip abroad. I know there are plenty of people who don't believe in "mediums" or put any stock in the abilities of "empaths," (a person with the paranormal ability to apprehend the mental or emotional state of another individual), but I can tell you without a doubt that what this person was able to tell me, as well as other people who were with me in Italy, was 100% genuine. There was no way he could have spoken these truths if he hadn't divined them from beyond this earthly plateau. I fully believe in divine intervention, and I was certain that going on that trip was an example of such providence meant to keep me on the path upon which I was meant to remain the rest of my life.

Granted, in some way each of the people on this trip were looking to find some type of peace in their lives, including myself. Many of us had gone through some tremendous recent tragedy, and this excursion was a way for us to seek and find peace. I recall the day that we were on the top of this beautiful mountainside in the presence of a statue of the blessed Mother Mary. A few steps in front of her, I knelt down to pray and felt something come over me. It felt like an embrace of pure love. The love of a mother. My own mother took a photo of me at that moment. My back was to her and I was on my knees praying to Mother Mary to help me help my children get through this difficult time as well as help me find my way out of the darkened recesses of my own mind.

Looking back at that moment, it must have been extremely agonizing for my mother to watch her own child languishing in so much heartache and pain, at the mercy of prayer before the feet of the statue of the Blessed Mother. As mothers, we all want to take the pain from our children and bear it upon our own shoulders, even though this is a burden that needs to be carried individually by each of us.

Many of the people on this trip began as strangers to each other, but by the end we all seemed to become a unified force of strength for each other, each having a role somehow in healing the others who needed healing. Helping each other to "un-numb" the pain and to find a way to peace. It was an incredibly emotional and spiritually enlightening trip, and I will be forever grateful that I had the opportunity to share it with my mother.

Chapter 8   **ANGER**

"Where there is hatred, let me sow love. Where there is injury, pardon. Where there is doubt, faith." ~ St. Francis of Assisi

Anger really is, as they say, an all-consuming fire. It only destroys. Anger slowly kills you and everyone around you. It eats at your soul. But it is real. It is tangible. I was so angry that I didn't know who to be angry with, so I began to feel anger towards practically everybody. Hate and bitterness built up inside me and I took offense to everything. I was putting up an invisible wall around anything that had to do with Michael. I had it in my mind that no else could grieve for my husband but me. They didn't have the right. I didn't want anyone to make it about them because I felt it wasn't about them. It was about my girls and me.

Then, I had an amazing breakthrough one day while in my therapist's office, and I just broke down sobbing into a pillow and I said, "I AM THE VICTIM HERE! NOT MICHAEL!" That was the first time that I said those words out loud, and I realized that it was Michael who I was angry with. It felt like the ultimate betrayal. I was suddenly directing all my anger back onto him because HE left us. HE LEFT US to pick up all these pieces. Shattered pieces of devastation.

It was a revelation. It made me think about the emotion of anger that was tearing me apart inside. With this understanding, I could begin to heal, because I could not be angry with Michael. How could I be angry with him? If he was really himself, he would have never taken himself away from his wife and children, leaving us in a wake of pain and devastation. There was simply no way. However, this stage of grief would be one that I would have to work through for quite a while. There was so much to be angry about and so many people to be angry with for a multitude of reasons.

For many, being angry is more acceptable than being sad. Sadness comes from hurt, and we don't want to hurt anymore.

We fear exposing our vulnerability, so we lash out at those around us. The anger could be towards someone close to us or a total stranger.

In an article I read in eCondolence, titled *Second Stage of Grief: Anger*, they expressed the sentiment similarly; "There are times in the natural grieving process for the individual to feel frustrated, trapped, and hurt. It is common to have those churning emotions surface and be directed toward someone or something. When pain dominated the feelings, it is natural to look for someone to blame. Being angry is a way of releasing energy, of protesting a loss that does not make sense or seem fair. Even though deep down one understands that anger is not logical or justified, emotions are rarely logical. Once the individual has stopped denying the loss has occurred, the reality of the situation begins to set in, bringing additional confusion, frustration and pain. The mind and body begin to deflect the pain, expressing it instead as anger. On occasion the anger may in fact be aimed at the deceased loved one, emotionally distraught because they left us. Anger often is a cyclical process. One feels guilty for feeling angry, which of course only leads to feeling more anger."

I knew I could work this out in counseling and be a happier person once I let go of my anger. I have found that the importance of therapy, whether it is professional help, or however you are able to raise self-awareness, is essential to healing. It helped me continue to heal and work through so many emotions and situations that I knew I couldn't handle alone. I have learned that even if you have people who love you and are there for you, it can still be vital to have a professional, unbiased voice in your corner to help guide you through very difficult times.

I remember at the beginning there were people, some family, some friends, some that actually hadn't even seen Michael in years who said things to me like, "I wish I could have been there for him," or "Maybe if I lived closer, or was around more, he would have come and talked to me." Of all the insensitive things people have said to me after Michael's death, and believe me there were many, these are some of the examples that just "stung" me. How could someone actually say that to me? Michael talked to me, his wife, all the time and about everything. He didn't want to talk to anyone else in those last few days because he wasn't himself, and if he had been, then he would be here today. Period.

It's such a battle in my mind because I always replay things over and over in my head thinking, *what could I have missed?* The reality was that Michael and I grew up together, and we were together for over twenty years. If he told me something that he believed to be true, I would believe it also. I never had any reason to doubt him because he was never anything but an honest, loving, caring husband and father. It was only when I saw the change in him that an alarm sounded inside of me, but by then it was too late. There was no way he was going to go and tell someone else what was "really going on" in his mind because I don't believe he even knew. He believed what he was telling me, and ultimately, devastatingly enough, he believed that doing what he did was the best solution to whatever was happening to him. Unfortunately, I will never fully know what that was. It will be something I will just have to live with.

Early on I had so many emotions swirling around in my mind. The last thing that I wanted to think about was meeting someone, particularly someone Michael and I both knew. My confusion, guilt and anger were so consuming at times that it made it difficult to even think straight. I was ultimately able to battle through these emotions because the positivity that came from being with Dennis diminished any negativity.

Interestingly, later getting involved with someone we both knew made me feel comforted somehow. Michael actually knew Dennis better than I did because he was the one who always took Olivia to karate class, which Dennis taught. It was Dennis' karate school. I came to realize that I felt safe around him. It was very comforting, and I trusted him from the very start. I hadn't felt anything like that for any other man besides Michael, and initially I didn't want to feel that way about anyone else. But

Dennis was different. When we met, he became someone who brought light back to my life. He put laughter back into my heart and he began to help me get back part of myself that I had lost.

When Dennis came into my life, many people closest to me were beyond happy for me, but not everyone. When I heard the gossip, I couldn't believe that some people were talking about me in such disparaging ways just for being with Dennis. They were reacting as if I was cheating on my husband. It made no sense to me, but that didn't stop the flood of emotions which churned inside me as a result, and I wouldn't be able to be free of it for a long time. I began to feel such anger, and then guilt, which I wouldn't be able to free myself from for a long time, because I had to constantly defend myself for trying to live my life. That's really all I was trying to do; live.

What did these people want? It was as if I was being judged by what they thought I should be doing with my life. It was as if they thought it was okay for me to be grieving and alone, but it was not okay if I had someone in my life who made me happy again. It made no sense, but all I kept thinking about was my children, and after a while I didn't care what other people thought about me. I knew I had always been a good mother, a good wife, and I did everything I thought to be "right." What happened in my life, happened to me. It happened to my children. I didn't choose it. We didn't choose it nor could we change it. What we needed to do was get through it somehow. However, it seemed the more I tried to find happiness the more some people wanted to condemn me.

It was in therapy that I finally began to work through my feelings of anger and hatred. I realized that I needed to know that when people judged me, they were not defining me, they were defining themselves. They hadn't walked in my shoes and their opinions would not change my life for better or for worse. I was the only one who could. I needed to make my life better and the choices I made would achieve that. My choice was to be with Dennis. I was blessed to fall in love again and, three years after Michael's passing, marry him. I decided that living my life was

71

much more important than living a life other people, who were not significant to me, thought I should live.

It's important to realize that no one is in charge of your life but you. No one is in charge of your happiness but you. My main priority remains my childrens' well-being. I came to realize that my happiness had a direct influence on their emotional state. I wanted to be happy again, but I had no idea how to fully allow myself to do so for quite a while. Ultimately, I knew that when my children saw me at peace again and living a healthy life, then they, too, would begin to heal because they would see they had their mother back; the strong, happy, in control person that they needed in their lives. They had lost their dad. They weren't going to lose me, too.

The more I held onto the anger, the more I gave power to those people who wanted me to remain unhappy and alone. I realized, almost too late, that I had to let go of people, even the ones I was once close with, who I had once called friends but proved otherwise. True friends are people who build you up and want to see you happy. Not those who want to see you happy within their own parameters.

My experience has taught me a lot about friendship these last few years. I cannot change people's thoughts and opinions, and I no longer try to do so. My hope is that people will look more at themselves and how they too quickly judge things they do not fully understand. I understand now that anger doesn't solve anything. It can only destroy. I will no longer let it destroy me or those I love in its wake.

GUILT

My profound sense of guilt was something that took a very long time for me to get over. I blamed myself. I must have done something wrong, I thought. Certainly, I could have done something different, something that would have prevented Michael from doing what he did.

Besides being my husband, Michael was also my best friend. There was no one closer to him than me. How could I not

72

realize that something was this severely wrong? The last week of his life, I had to force him to speak to people because of how delusional and paranoid he had suddenly become. I was the only one that he trusted in those last days, and I felt that I failed in so many ways.

With a suicide, especially when there were never any signs or a diagnosis of depression, it is very hard to come to grips with it and find closure. The guilt consumes and makes it incredibly hard to move forward.

I suppose I will always wonder "what if." What if there was more that I could have done to help him sooner? When it finally seemed to click in my head that my husband really had something wrong, something going on in his mind that he couldn't control and I was going to take him to get him help, it was too late. This is a thought that, to some extent, continues to be forever etched in my mind. However, I now believe that for some reason I wasn't able to help him because that was the way that this life was planned. I remember not being able to make sense of what was happening on those last days. I couldn't understand some of the things that he was saying. His thoughts and words were just so out of his character, but it wasn't something that had been going on for very long. As I have called it, it was like my ten days of hell.

During that time, I didn't know what to do or who I could talk to about what I was seeing. I certainly didn't want to have my children see their father that way. Although I do know now that they did notice the sudden change in his personality, even if only in the subtlest of ways, but did not talk about it. At the time, they were consumed by grief over the loss of my grandmother, with whom my girls were very close. It was a very emotional time, and my own grief over her passing was what made me think "what did I miss?" after Michael's death. The guilt I felt over not being able to help prevent what happened to him is something that I still battle.

It was very hard for me to grasp the reality that there was nothing I could do to change what happened. I am the type of person that wants to be able to fix everything. If someone I love is hurting, I want to be able to fix it. When my children are going through pain or difficult times, I will do everything I can to make them feel better. I always try to make sure I am there for all my daughters, even though it is sometimes hard to do so. I was a single parent and I had to try to pick up the shattered pieces of our family and make us all whole again.

I have come to realize that I can only let my children know that I am there for them. I can only do my best because if you try to always please everyone at the same time it is a battle you cannot win. But for a long time, I wanted to try to win that battle because of all the trauma that they had endured. The thing was that we ALL endured this trauma together and we all dealt with recovering from it in different ways. Thankfully we have an army of people who love us, and my daughters know that they will always have someone they can turn to. And that's really the most important thing.

Annual Salem, MA Family Trip

Block Island, RI

Michael, Jackie & Victoria

Softball family picnic

Michael & Olivia

Walt Disney World

Jackie & Michael /Final travel softball game

Summer 2015

Michael & Olivia
First Communion

Victoria & Michael
Sports Award
Banquet

Beavertail Park Jamestown, RI

Praying for Peace
Italy, 2016

Christmas
Dominican Republic
2015

My mother and me

My father and me 1994

Mom & Rick

Amy,
me,
Ann,
Barbara

"The
Yaya's"

My niece
Brooklynn

My sister Erika & Steve

Dennis & Me

Our Engagement

Erika, Olivia,
Victoria, me, Jackie
& Brooklynn

Our Wedding

And Now these three remain:

Faith, Hope, Love

But the Greatest of These is Love. 1 Corinthians 13:13

"When you come out of the storm, you won't be the same person who walked in. That's what the storm is all about."

~ Haruki Murakami

Beavertail State Park, Jamestown RI
Photo by: Bethany Steere

Chapter 9 **MEDIUMS, PSYCHICS AND DREAMS**

"Cherish your visions and your dreams as they are the children of your soul, the blueprints of your ultimate achievements." ~Napoleon Hill

I do not believe that this life is all there is, and while I have always believed that there are "gifted" people who are sensitive to that higher level of existence, including my own mother, Michael did not have the same belief, at least until the day he attended a friend's parent's funeral. Both Michael's own parents were deceased, and he never went to the cemetery because he felt that they weren't there, but that their spirits were with us.

After Michael returned home from this funeral, my mother told me that she had seen a vision of Michael's father at the cemetery with his arms wrapped around his own gravestone. I knew that he had gone to the funeral, but I did not realize he had gone to his parents' gravesites.

"Michael, my mother wanted me to tell you about a vision she had about your dad," I said, and then told him about my mother's vison. Does that make sense?"

"Yes, I was there today," he said in a shocked tone. When my mother mentioned the name of the person who passed and that person's relatives, pretty much listing the whole family, it changed Michael's thinking about my mother's psychic ability forever because that day he had been at the cemetery where his mother and father were buried. Ironically, it would be the precise spot where his own life would end approximately fifteen years later.

After Michael's death, desperate to hear something from him that I could use to hang on to hope that he was in a better place, I would go to certain mediums. I believed that they were able to channel Michael through them. One medium in particular even took on his personality and told me things only Michael would know, and it made me feel better in some way.

83

One well-known psychic told me that Michael was showing a ring, and that he was congratulating me. But I wasn't with anyone, and the farthest thing from my mind was being married again. The thought alone actually upset and angered me. After the show, the psychic spoke to me alone, which was something that I found astonishing. He was a world-renowned psychic, and it was kind of crazy that he felt compelled enough to try to give me this message. He told me that there was someone that I already knew in some capacity, and that this person and I were supposed to be together. He also said that I was going to try to push this person away, but that I should not. He told me that this would be a 'very viable relationship.'

I couldn't stand to even think of something like that at the time. It was a very difficult for me to think of anything other than the pain and confusion I was feeling. All I wanted was answers to what happened; what happened to him that drove him to do what he did or what had gone so wrong so quickly. This psychic told me that something just "went off" in Michael's head. He told me it happened quickly, and there was nothing I could have done to stop it.

However, I needed more than that. To me, it was not an answer, but I knew I had to come to terms with the reality that I would never get those questions answered, and that may have been the hardest thing to accept.

There was another medium, also quite well known, whom I had gone to see on numerous occasions over the past few years. I had gone to see him just after Michael passed with my mother and sister. The medium was speaking at a public event, a small venue of about 40 people or so. Before the show, he always writes down a number of messages onto sheets of paper. They are communications that he had channeled from people who had passed on, and they are later presented to specific audience members who had lost someone. There are stacks of these sheets of paper, and some of them are delivered to people in the audience, some are not. Everyone in the room wants to connect to their loved ones in some way, and everyone hopes that they will

84

receive a sheet of paper from the medium with a message from a loved one on it.

Over time I have received eight such pieces of paper with notes from Michael. He always comes through very strong with specific messages. They are always messages that only myself or people close to Michael would know.

That first night I had gone to see him I had no idea what to expect. I was already feeling very emotional when I caught a glimpse of the first paper with *Michael* written on it.

"There is a male here with me who committed suicide," the medium said.

I lost my breath for a moment, and then I started sobbing uncontrollably. The medium came right over to me and said, "He says he is so sorry for what he did." He then went on to talk to me for quite some time. He told me that Michael knew I was wearing his chain. And I was. I had on the gold chain and the medallion of St. Michael that my husband had worn each day and night since I met him. The medallion was what I bought him on our first anniversary.

St. Michael the Archangel was the protector. Now I was wearing it praying for protection from the unrelenting pain and suffering we were all going through. My clothes were covering it completely and it could not be seen, so the medium asked me if I was wearing it.

What happened next took me by complete surprise. The medium basically started taking on Michael's mannerisms. He grabbed my shoulders and said, "I love you so much. I love you so much." He also said, "I found grandma."

I was shocked by all this. My grandmother died just four days before him. It was an incredibly profound experience.

I had actually received two papers that night. One said, *I'm sorry about the gun.* The other one said, *Michael is so sorry that he did what he did. He wanted to get it cleared up but he couldn't, and that "my head doesn't hurt anymore. You were so good to me.*"

It was almost more than I could bear. I felt so many conflicting emotions. I suppose in some way I felt a peacefulness because I had a way of knowing that he was still with us. It is something that I believe with every part of me. I believe that our loved ones are always with us, and I completely believe they can give us signs in different forms, including through mediums.

I remember one day that was within the first week or two of Michael's passing. I kept "talking" to Michael that day. I always talked to him. Sometimes out loud in my car and sometimes in my head. This particular day I got very angry, and I said, "Everyone talks about signs. Where are my signs? I want a sign, and don't give me a just a penny or a rock."

I was literally telling my deceased husband what kind of signs I wanted, and that I wouldn't be satisfied with anything small. I can look back on that now and laugh a little, but at the time I really meant it. And as crazy as it may seem, I got a sign from him that day. I was in this big waiting room, waiting for my appointment time when I suddenly spotted a quarter near my feet. I just knew this was a sign. I picked it up. The date on it was 1968; Michael's birth year. So, it seemed Michael had heard my rant earlier and obliged me by sending a sign he knew I would be looking for, even if I wanted something more out of the ordinary. When I told the medium about the quarter when I went in to see him a short time later, he made a comment and laughed, saying that Michael says, "She wants me to send her big signs, but I'm not that good at it yet."

That did make me smile.

HIDDEN MEANINGS AND FAMILY MEMORIES

I now find myself living through signs often, especially significant numbers that I take notice of, like birthdays on license plates, dates on coins or various signs in nature. I believe that seeing cardinals are signs of our deceased loved ones coming to us to show us that they are near. I am sure plenty of people will think this is sheer lunacy. However, it is something that brings me solace.

When we moved into our new home after Michael passed, the first warm spring day I went to sit out on the back steps with a cup of coffee. Staring out at the trees around the large back yard, I saw butterflies fluttering and heard the sound of the birds chirping, which I always loved hearing, and felt something truly special taking place. Then, I spotted the most beautiful cardinal perched on the fence. I had never really seen many cardinals before I moved to this house, but this one sat there for a while, and then each day for some time after that I would see a cardinal, or sometimes more than one, in the yard. Many times, I would just stop and listen to them chirping, captivated by the distinct, beautiful songs they sang, communicating with one another in this secret musical language. It gave me such a feeling of peace, like I was being watched over from above.

Often, when I am listening to the radio, I hear specific songs that remind me not only of Michael, but of my grandparents and other loved ones. Whenever I hear *Sorento* by Mario Lanza, I always think of my grandfather. I am the oldest of two children, and the eldest granddaughter on both my mother and father's side. My mother comes from a large Italian family of nine brothers and sisters, and I was not only the oldest grandchild, but I was alone in my spoiled freedom for three years before my next cousin was born. Still, I would be the only girl for the next six years until my sister was born. I was sort of the princess, which, make no mistake about it, I loved. My grandfather even called me *Princess Pocahontas* because I had long, dark hair and olive skin. He would always affectionately say that I tanned as soon as the sun came out.

I have a cousin, Scott, three years younger than I, who today I like to call my little brother. When we were growing up, we would fight as if we were actually siblings, with my little brother pestering me. We loved each other, but that didn't prevent all the teasing and fighting, which I never got blamed for because in my grandfather's eyes I could do no wrong. My cousin will be the first to remind me of this to this day. It was pretty funny. Although maybe not to my cousin, but we have a lot of great memories. I spent most of the summer at my grandparents' house. There were always a lot of kids in the neighborhood. We would be outside from morning until the street light came on, only coming in for lunch. With no cell phones or electronics like there are today, we were constantly busy riding bikes or playing manhunt, kickball, street hockey, and every possible game you could think of. It was just a different generation. I wish my daughters could have had these experiences without all the social pressure, living through social media and being "connected" twenty-four hours a day.

My youngest, Olivia, had gone to camp for a couple of years and she was the first of my daughters to do so. I thought it would be a good opportunity for her, and when she was twelve, she went to an overnight camp for a week. There were no cell phones allowed and they spent the time doing different activities and getting to know the other campers. Old school, right? To everyone's surprise, including her own, she absolutely loved it and I was thrilled. The thing that she had been most afraid of was giving up her dependence on technology, and it turned out that she didn't miss it the way she thought she would. In fact, she found the experience of being "off the grid" both liberating and fulfilling. She liked camp so much that the following year she decided to go for two weeks. It might be the only way for her to understand a little of what it was like during my childhood. Just being allowed to be a kid and have fun seems so simple, but unfortunately that innocence seems lost in some ways on children today, and on society as a whole.

I have so many incredible memories of my grandfather and my grandmother, who he called Busy Bee because she was just that, always busy doing something, whether it was cooking, cleaning, or tending to children; she never stopped. I have fond memories of my grandparents' home growing up. There was always something going on and people coming in and out of the house. It was loud, but in a fun, familiar and comforting way, and there was always a lot of food, which may have been why there were always people coming in and out. It was in the comfort and security of this environment that I grew up, and it shaped the woman I am today. It influenced the wife and mother that I became and built the foundations of the ethical and moral ideologies that I developed in my life. Sadly, my grandfather passed when I was sixteen-years old. He was sick often in his life, and I remember him being in and out of the hospital for heart and other health issues. My grandmother passed earlier in the same year that Michael passed, ironically the same year as my grandmother on my father's side.

I have dreams of them often, and many times I hear them call my name, and sometimes it's as if I can feel them hugging me without saying a word. My belief is that they still watch over us even though they are not here. I know that the love we share with our loved ones will never die, and I believe that at those times when we feel most lost is when our lost loved ones try to find ways to let us know that they have never left us.

My family has had a big influence on me. I grew up with a lot of love and support, and I realize now I was very fortunate. We certainly did have our share of heartache because when you come from a large family, although there may be a lot of love that gets shared, there is unavoidable heartache that gets shared as well. Many loved ones were lost over the years, and some long before their time. We held each other up through it all, and were blessed to have such a strong and loving family unit. Sometimes it felt like an army fighting beside you, like on the tragic day that Michael passed. My whole family came together to be there because this was something we did; going through the pain of loss together. I believe that if I didn't have all the support and love that my family provided, not only during this most tragic time but during my entire life, I wouldn't be person that I am today. I know that is something that has guided me, and continues to guide me, keeping me strong even on the days when I think that strength is the last thing I have.

Chapter 10   **A LOOK BACK**

"My past has not defined me, destroyed me, deterred me, or defeated me; it has only strengthened me." ~ Steve Maraboli

I believe that how we are brought up is what ultimately shapes the way we face and perceive life. When I was a little girl, I had a plaque on my wall with the poem, *Children Learn What They Live* by Dorothy Law Nolte 1972. This poem states, among other things, that if children live with criticism, they learn to condemn. If children live with hostility they learn to fight. It goes on to speak of many of the negatives that a child may live with, and the consequences. It also speaks of the positives. If children live with encouragement, they learn confidence. If children live with security, they learn to have faith in themselves and in those around them.

I remember reading this poem even before I could actually understand the true dynamic of it. Because my life was filled with love and caring, I grew up with that security. I grew up with very strong people. Ever since I can remember, my father was always a strong man both physically and mentally. He battled cancer more than once in his life, the first time when he was just 38 years old. He was diagnosed with Non-Hodgkin's lymphoma. The doctors had given him only three months to live if the chemotherapy and radiation didn't work, and he was given a massive amount of both. The incredible thing about this is that I have no memory of him being sick during the time he was fighting cancer. This was because he did not allow me to see it. He never complained or even talked about any of the pain or anxiety or anything else that may have been bothering him. I don't remember him ever being sick in bed from any reason. Not ever. My mother was the same way. I remember going to the hospital to see him once during this time and he made sure that he wasn't in hospital clothes. He changed into his jeans and shirt before we got there. He never wanted my sister and I to worry about him or be afraid that he would die. We never knew until much later just how sick he really was. When I look back and see some of the pictures of him during that time, it shocks me because he was very frail looking, with dark circles under his eyes and hair that was very thin, when normally he had a thick head of black hair. I suppose you can say that we see what we wish to see in life. I chose to not see my father as sick, even if there was every indication that he was. I wouldn't let my mind go there.

Then I look back and see my mother doing whatever she could in her power to shield us from feeling the pain that she must have been feeling, having no idea where her life was heading. The doctors had told her to prepare herself because her husband's cancer would most likely kill him, and she had two daughters, age 6 and 12, who could be losing their father. Somehow, she managed to hold it all together, while at the same time running a business as well as the household, cooking and cleaning and driving my sister and me to school or wherever else we needed to be. Throughout it all, she never faltered or let us see her break down in any way.

Having children of my own, and not wanting to see them ever hurt, I understand the desire of any mother to carry the full burden for their children while putting on a brave face. I remember only once seeing my mother cry outwardly during my father's illness, and it occurred when she was talking to one of the priests in church while my sister and I were attending a small Catholic elementary school in Providence. My mother and her whole family had attended the church and school, which was in the same neighborhood where she grew up. While confiding in the priest about my father's condition, she suddenly started crying.

NO PLAN B

After fighting the toughest battle of his life to date, my father's cancer went into remission. I suppose you can say that he wasn't ready for this to be *the last bell* for him. It was truly miraculous, and it continues to amaze people to this day when they hear his story. Today he is seventy-one years old and going strong. I tell him all the time to slow down, but he just laughs and says, "I will soon." He's been saying that for over twenty years. It's not his way. And that just makes him who he is, who he has always been, and that's ok. Just as the tattoo he has on his arm states; *There is No Plan B,* which refers to the fact that if the cancer were to come back, the way he lived his life would not change, he would continue to do things his way until the end. This philosophy underscores the reality that we really have nothing if we don't have our health.

However, as far as all other aspects and areas of our lives, we must be willing to have a plan B. And C. And D. If your world suddenly changes and forces you to look at your life and say, "Now what do I do?" you will be overwhelmed and lost with seemingly no way out. Or you may just find yourself having to make a decision to change some particular aspect of your life, regardless of what it might be. Sometimes there are situations beyond our control that force us to look at another way of life. This could be with any area in life, such as relationships, career, education, or where you reside. Taking the first steps always seem to be the most difficult, but once you let go of the fear and apprehension you may find that your situation is exactly where you are meant to be on your life's journey. Plan B may not have been your first choice, but it is sometimes necessary, and in the end it can still be beautiful.

STRENGTH OF WOMEN

I come from a long line of strong women, from my mother to my grandmothers and even my great-grandmothers, from the stories that I have heard. I will forever feel the strength of my grandmothers throughout my life. I think of them often, particularly during the most difficult and trying times in my life. I feel that there are messages in every thought I have of them. There are lessons that I have taken from each of them which have shaped much of who I am today.

During my childhood, my parents owned a jewelry manufacturing business where I spent a lot of time after school. They started the company operating out of a small one-room building, and it grew from there. This was during the 1970's and

80's, when the industry was still in its prime, before most jewelry production was outsourced overseas and a long-time staple in the Rhode Island economy was lost forever. I can vividly recall the huge factory in Providence where my parent's business thrived, at a time when the booming jewelry industry stimulated the state's economy and the city was vibrant and alive.

My father named the company after the street he grew up on, the street where my grandmother lived for over fifty years. The house was a red brick cape built in 1948, the same year my father was born. My grandmother was so proud of that house because it was the first one on the street. She and my grandfather had three children together but divorced when my father and his sister and brother were still young. My grandmother would remain in the house with the children until each grew up and went on their own. That house, as well as my mother's parent's house, will forever be the memories of my childhood that I continue to look back on most fondly. I can still recall everything about the house and the yard from all the time I spent there while growing up. The side and backyard were not very large, but when you are little everything seem so much bigger. There was a large tree out back that provided a lot of shade, and several smaller fruit trees; pear, apple and cherry trees. In the very corner of the back yard was my favorite; the lilac tree. When it bloomed in the spring the smell would intoxicate me.

I recall walking into the small first floor bathroom with the black and white checkered floor and opening up the medicine cabinet and seeing a black tube of lipstick. It was Revlon and it was the deepest red color. I was about 9, and while I was putting that lipstick on my lips, I remember feeling so glamorous. Then I heard my grandmother yell, "Janine, what are you doing?"

"Nothing, grandma," I said as I hurriedly tried to scrub the lipstick off my lips so I wouldn't get into trouble.

I can still see my reflection in the mirror. To this day, I find myself bringing up my grandmother's "Revlon Red."

She was a loving woman, but she was definitely strict. She would always let my sister and I help her put the laundry on the clothesline, which extended from the bathroom window to the tree into the backyard. I loved helping her with this chore and the smell of the white cotton sheets and towels drying freshly on the line in the warm summer sun. Because of this experience, fresh white cotton sheets remain one of favorite things.

She was forever cooking and baking. She loved making new things for us try. I especially remember all the food she baked. I never had much of a sweet-tooth, preferring chips and salty snacks over the chocolate and baked goods. However, my favorite baked good that she made, which I have finally perfected on my own, is lemon meringue pie. It took me forever to learn how to make the foamy peaks as high as she did without it flopping down into a deflated sorrowful sight. The first time I achieved this I felt sheer pride. It is a delicious testament to my grandmother's love.

My grandmother on my mother's side, although different, was like my other grandmother in the fact that I learned a lot from her, as well. My maternal grandmother was a lot less strict with us. She would joke around and liked to make us laugh. She, too, was always cooking, only for many more people. Having nine children, the family was continually growing as more grandchildren were added over the years, and she cooked for all of them. Her house was never without grandchildren. My favorite food was her eggplant and her Italian egg biscuits she made for Easter. I now make each of these things all the time and think of her.

A story she used to enjoy telling people were the times when I was young and I would tell her to take her coffee and sit outside while I cleaned the house for her. It didn't matter that she couldn't find half of her things after I cleaned. She would laugh about it. I just loved to make everything look nice.

One important thing she always told me that I will never forget was, "Don't wait to do things. That time may not come."

She would say that she and my grandfather would always talk about taking trips and going places when the kids got older, or when this happens, or that happens, but they never got a chance to do the things they talked about because he died in his sixties and she went to live on without him for the next twenty-five years.

In other words, never put off for tomorrow what you can do today.

If it's within your means, just do it. I always at least try to live my life this way. Between my grandmothers and my mother, who was always one of my biggest rocks and supporters my whole life, I learned more life lessons through these incredible, strong women than I could ever learn from reading any book or taking any class. I try to remember all the incredible things they taught me each day, which especially come shining through during my darkest days. It took everything I had in me to harness their strength through some of the days when I felt I could no longer make it. Because I am imbued with the spirit and strength of these incredible women, I was able to persevere and overcome any hardship.

Chapter 11 STIGMA, CURIOSITY & CONCERN
"Not all wounds are visible."

I've come to learn that there is a fine line between curiosity and concern. When a person dies, no matter what age they are when they pass, there are people left behind that love them and feel the loss. There are also those that feel empathy for the ones who are going through the loss. These people of compassion could be family members, close friends or even strangers. Their genuine feelings make the bereaved feel better as they go through the grieving process.

People are curious by nature, and when someone passes unexpectedly, especially someone young, they always want to know what happened. When someone dies from an illness or an accident or some natural cause it is still, of course, tragic and difficult. However, when the word *suicide* is whispered, the premature and unnatural death takes on a whole new connotation.

When a loved one takes their own life, how does anyone respond to the question, "How did your husband or father, in the case of my children, die?"

How do I answer that question? Am I supposed to answer it just as I might have if it had been cancer or an accident?

"Oh, he shot himself."

If I do actually tell the truth about how he died, it's never enough for some people. They always look at you as if they want to hear more. What everyone wants to know, besides how the act was done, is, "Why did he do it?" That's a question that I still cannot answer.

Other causes of death typically do not require further explanation, but in the silence that follows the information that your loved one killed themselves is the implication that you did something to cause it or did not do enough to prevent it.

This was just one of the many difficult things surrounding Michael's passing that I struggled with for a long time. Life was

96

really just beginning for us, the pieces falling into place, everything making sense, and then without warning he was gone. It will probably always be difficult for my children and myself to explain to someone how he died. It really does feel like it's always the subject of explanation. It just doesn't seem fair.

It's not easy to put into words, but when the question comes up, and it will always come up, there is no discernable answer that my daughters and I will be able to provide that won't result in the look of confusion or shock on the face of the curious person inquiring about the nature of Michael's passing.

It's true; this was not a "typical death." Death is sad, but it is typically not shockingly gruesome or violent. At least not in my life experience. That is one of the major reasons I chose to write this book. I didn't write it to become famous or rich, or anything like that. I wrote it to shed light on many aspects of the most difficult time in my life and my family's life, as well as to help and inform others going through the loss of a loved one or similar situation. I am putting my most personal thoughts and emotions out there for everyone to see, exposing a raw and vulnerable side of my personal life to people who know me and total strangers alike. I am inviting anyone and everyone into my world and the lives of my family because I feel that this is a story of importance for several reasons. I want people to know the remarkable person, caring husband and loving father who was Michael Passaretti, but I also want people who are going through a similar tragedy in their lives to know that there are ways to find hope through the darkness. No matter how many times you may fall, the important thing is to keep getting back up.

We all know people who have gone through loss, and the pain that I personally have gone through isn't any worse than the pain experienced by anyone else who has lost a loved one, it is just different. Every situation is different. When it comes to suicide, however, there is a stigma attached. You can usually tell by the discernable gasp that follows the very utterance of the word. I suppose my daughters and I will be better able to handle a discussion of this topic the more time goes by, but there will always be that stigma.

MENTAL ILLNESS

For many people, mental illness is synonymous with words like "madness," "insanity," "lunacy," and evokes images of padded cells, caretakers in white suits, and straitjackets. However, people with mental disorders are not raving maniacs. Nor are people with odd personalities or idiosyncrasies mentally ill. Mental illness is complex, and it is not always easy to identify, as each disorder involves a cluster of symptoms, which often overlap. If you want to look at schizophrenia, that might be the biggest mystery of all. Schizophrenia is a devastating mental illness that afflicts 1% of the population worldwide, including many veterans. People suffering with schizophrenia experience such disruptive symptoms as hallucinations, delusions of persecution, disorganized thinking, and the even more disabling negative symptoms, which include loss of interest in other people as well as their own self-care. While schizophrenia has long been known to run in families, it has only been in the last few years that scientists have reliably identified specific genetic changes thought to increase susceptibility to schizophrenia. Most of these changes in the genetic code, or mutations, have very small effects individually, but can act together to significantly increase the risk of becoming ill.

I can't say any of this has to do with Michael's case, but to this day it is difficult for my children and I to fathom that a perfectly happy, healthy man who was never depressed a day in his life could have something go so wrong in his mind, and so quickly that he would take his own life. It doesn't make sense to us, or anyone that knew him well, because Michael had never displayed any signs or symptoms of any kind of mental illness previous to his behavior during those last couple weeks of his life. Mental illness is not something you can catch like a cold. It's very scary to think that this is something that could happen to anyone at any time.

I wish we could escape the stigma of suicide, not only

because of how it makes us feel when we see the reaction from people, but because I never want people to think that Michael was a selfish person; someone who consciously took himself away from his family.

This is often something I hear when I am either reading or watching something on television about those who commit suicide. Often, they are talked about as being selfish. That they didn't consider the ones they left behind in pain. I know in my heart, and with everything inside me, that his girls and I were the most important things in his life. Like the tattoo of the earth he had on his calf with the words, *My World*, along with names of his daughters and me orbiting around it. He was never a man who put himself before his family. Whatever happened in his mind led him to believe that this was the only decision he had. This is a thought that will never cease from our minds. The thought of *what* exactly was going through his mind and why he never said anything about it to us. Not ever.

Tragically, whatever happened to him happened so quickly that any signs indicating he might be headed down such a dark road became evident too late. It was as if something alien took over him, and then he was gone.

I can only hope that if a person or a loved one is going through something similar involving any form of depression or anxiety, they seek immediate help in some way. There are some things that we just cannot fix on our own. We may even feel that something not-quite-right is going on, and we brush it off thinking it will just go away. Or maybe people will say something along the lines of, "Get over it, you'll be fine," or "It will pass."

If someone is in the middle of depression, or any kind of pain, we need to be there for them any way that we can, especially if they verbalize it to us. In Michael's case, we weren't given the chance to help. I believe he thought he could "fix" whatever it was that he was feeling, but it proved too much for him to handle alone. We will never know the true extent of the pain he was suffering, but knowing him the way I did and seeing his personality change so drastically so quickly, I don't believe it was something he was able to control. I knew him so well that if he spoke just one word out of character, it would have raised a red flag for me, and that was exactly what happened in those last days.

There may not be much that I can do to erase the stigma of suicide, but my hope is that our story may provide insight to others and help people before they turn to suicide.

There isn't always an answer, and you can't just assign blame to loved ones or even directly on the person who took their own life. The many myths associated with suicide contribute significantly to the stigma. The notion that people who kill themselves are "selfish" or "weak" continues to persist today, and it needs to stop. The loved ones who didn't see the signs aren't "stupid" or "careless". These are all things that I have heard many times. The survivors of suicide loss may always wonder if we might have contributed in some way to the actions of their deceased loved one, but in our fragile states of mourning, we as the survivors have to come to terms with the perceptions of what the rest of society may be thinking about us, and move on. So deep runs the guilt and self-blame that I only pray society becomes more educated and enlightened about it so that judgements and criticism and preaching uneducated and ignorant views about what we don't understand becomes a thing of the past.

Chapter 12   **LEARNING TO LOVE AGAIN**

"God can restore what is broken and change it into something amazing. All you need is faith." ~Joel 2:25

After Michael's passing, the days were long and arduous, and at night it felt like I was being pulled into an eternal abyss of darkness. A darkness that no one could possibly fathom. I could not escape my dark thoughts, reliving the nightmare over and over in my mind. The lingering and menacing questions I could not answer; *Who was I now* and *What will become of my children and me?*

In an instant, without warning, without reason, the life my children and I knew was ripped from us and we were left alone. My children were without their father, and I did not have my husband. My incredibly whole and happy family was gone. I didn't know who I was anymore. I went from being someone who was happily married, just beginning the middle of a life with three young daughters, to a single mother and a widow. I was becoming an empty shell of the person I used to be and I had no idea what life was going to become for us. The struggle to survive the overwhelming grief and emotions of confusion, guilt, debilitating sadness, PTSD, while trying to sustain and rebuild a life was some days close to impossible. There were days I didn't think I was going to survive let alone be happy again.

However, it seemed God and the universe had other plans for me. I believe the same is true for each and every one of us. No matter what you believe is supposed to happen, or what direction you think your life should take, fate may have something entirely different in store for you.

DENNIS

I was never one to believe in coincidences and "random occurrences." There are so many things that happen in life that have led me to my belief otherwise, and it became abundantly apparent to me when Dennis entered my life that some things are meant to be.

At an age when Olivia was considering what sports she wanted to play, or what social activities she wanted to get involved in, a family acquaintance suggested the possibility of karate, and very highly recommended, Dennis Molloy, a friend who ran a karate school. He had been involved in karate for over 30 years, proudly earning his eighth-degree black belt during our relationship, as well as winning a world championship in Ireland in 2011 at age 49.

Olivia gave it a try and immediately loved it, as well as Dennis, who was great with the kids. I saw right away that he was extremely dedicated, focused and he cared greatly about all his students. She thrived in this environment and progressed rather quickly, winning her first tournament at the age of 10. She was still taking classes when our world was shattered by Michael's death. Dennis contacted me a day later with his most sincere condolences.

Like everyone who knew Michael, Dennis was shocked and saddened by the tragedy. He also called to tell me that Olivia had signed up for a special event at his karate school, and he expressed that he would still love to have her participate if she was up to it. Even if it only took her mind off the sheer horror of losing her father for a short while, he wanted her to be able to do this, and offered to help in any way he could.

Olivia did go to the event, with Dennis keeping her under his "protective wing" all night. He was able to talk to her for a little while, and he even took her with him to pick up the pizza for the event. She was so broken. I saw pictures from that night, and all I could see was my little eleven-year old girl who always had a smile on her face, now so full of sadness. A carefree and happy childhood was cut way too short. It was heartbreaking to see, but I was truly grateful that Dennis, as well as all the friends she made at his school, were there for her at this time.

Over the next eight or so months, we were all just trying to survive, fighting our daily battles, one excruciating second at a time. Things we once loved took a backseat for my children and me. This included karate for Olivia, but even as her interest began to wane, I kept in contact with Dennis. We both really wanted to get her back to her routine. We tried, but it proved difficult, and there weren't many days I could get her to go. It was understandable, yet sad, but we never gave up.

For me, I found writing in a journal therapeutic, a way to release an assortment of pent-up emotions. What I was journaling were mainly feelings of debilitating sadness, and the feeling that any indication of the happy and whole person I once had been was retreating further and further away, becoming a distant memory. I found that it would comfort me to write in my journal while sitting by the ocean. If there was ANY form of peace (definitely a word that was becoming foreign to me), I would find it near the ocean. Beavertail in Jamestown is a place that I was very connected with because Michael and I took the girls there all the time to fly kites, throw the softball around, sit and relax and enjoy family life.

Coincidentally, Dennis also had a personal connection with Beavertail, which I learned about after spending an afternoon there by myself one day in late May 2016. I posted a photo of myself there with my journal on Facebook, and that evening Dennis sent me a message via FB that he has also been at Beavertail alone earlier that same day. We were both there, though on opposite sides of the park at the same time, he on the East and me on the West, doing our own individual soul-searching and trying to find some peace within ourselves. This twist of fate was a major catalyst that helped to eventually bring the two of us together.

A STEP FORWARD TOGETHER

After that, we began to talk via text more regularly, still without any thoughts of this being anything more than a friendship. We were allies trying to bring Olivia back into the karate studio. I found it comforting to talk to him, never awkward or forced. Then, we made plans to have lunch or dinner together. At the time, I did not have any pretenses about it, just spending some time together to talk. While I felt comfortable enough with Dennis, when that night came, I also felt somewhat uneasy because this was the first time that I had been out to dinner with someone other than Michael in over twenty years and I couldn't completely get rid of the guilt I felt just being with him. Another part of me battled against the defense.

Was I meant to walk alone the rest of this life?

Part of me did conceive that losing Michael meant just that. Yet once again, I felt that God and Universe had another plan for me.

I was experiencing many different emotions over this situation, but I definitely realized that my feelings for Dennis were more than just that of friends, and it was apparent that he felt the same way. This was the beginning of a new, wonderful, and fulfilling, if sometimes daunting relationship that would change everything in my world and my childrens' world. It was like being on the biggest, scariest rollercoaster ride of my life, but one in which was made bearable because Dennis was on the ride right beside me the entire time.

We began to spend more time together, just going for drives and talking. We learned more about each other with each passing day, and it was clear that our lives were different in many ways. I was a widow, married for twenty years and raising three children, while Dennis did not have children. He was divorced, having been previously married for a short time twenty-five years before. Regardless of these differences and our individual experiences, we loved sharing our stories with each other, revealing everything that made us who we were. It was exciting for me to listen to his stories about traveling the karate circuit and competing for world titles. He lights up when he talks about the day that he won the WAKO (World Association of Kickboxing Organization) World Championship in Ireland in 2011 and the pride he felt for the United States when he was on the podium and they played the national anthem. He worked extremely hard establishing an amazing karate career and opening his own karate studio in 1981. It makes me so proud when we walk into karate events and everyone knows him and makes it a point to come up and say hello. You can tell he is very respected, not just for what he has accomplished in his karate career but. more importantly, who he is as a person. Many people address him as *Master*, or *Shihan,* which is a term used in many Japanese martial arts as an honorific title for a senior expert or master instructor. It's very honoring and well-deserved because of his lifelong dedication, however, I always jokingly tell him, "I'm sorry, but I draw the line on calling you, Master." He shrugs and laughs every time I lovingly call him *Master Shifu,* who is the Kung Fu Master in the childrens' movie *Kung Fu Panda.* He actually gets a pretty big kick out of that one.

We made each other laugh, and continue to do so. When we talked about certain topics, Dennis seemed to always have specifics about the subject, no matter what it was. It would go something like, "Did you know that many of the stars we are looking at don't even exist any longer. They are so distant that their light may have shined millions of years ago and it took this long for it to reach us, so when we are looking deep into space it's like looking into the past."

However impressed, I would laugh and say he was like a walking *Wikipedia* page. I would joke with him, asking him for a "fun fact for the day."

He always obliged. He helped me to express a lot of what I was feeling, struggling as a single parent to raise my girls. I wanted to do whatever I could to make their lives easier, all while dealing with my own deep grief. It was far from easy, and I often sat and wondered why he would want to come into such a heavy situation, but I was glad he was there. He did everything he could to show me that he wanted to be there, and that he had no intention of going anywhere. It was definitely an internal battle that I needed to work through in my own mind with Dennis walking by my side through it all.

This was obviously going to be a very unconventional relationship right from the beginning. How other people felt about my relationship with Dennis was another matter, but there was no way that I could be seen by my children having someone else other than Michael in my life so soon after his death, even though I was sure they didn't want to see me wandering the rest of my life down the lonely, depressed and faltering path that I had been traveling. Dennis gave me a sense of calm, which came over me whenever we were together. A peacefulness that I so desperately needed.

Dennis entering my life was the beginning of my emergence from the storm. Being with him helped change so much for me, and I began to see my life differently. I was entering the second part of my life, moving from what my life was like before the tragedy to life after the tragedy.

MOVING FORWARD DESPITE JUDGEMENT

It was a time of renewed happiness for me, but again, it was also a time that completely began to change the way some people looked at me. While those closest to me were happy for me because they had seen me for so long losing myself and my will to live, it was shocking to see and hear some of the reactions of the people who judged me for what developed between Dennis and me and questioned my love for Michael. It had been eight months since Michael's death, but it seemed much longer to me, and when the friendship I had with Dennis developed into something more, it seemed right. Time was relative. He was someone that I felt had been put into my life for a reason. I was desperately trying to come out of the darkness and despair, but I didn't know how. Dennis helped me to do that. I call him my soldier because I feel he marched through hell by my side, repeatedly fighting a battle to help me find my way through the devastation. The battle to help me find myself. He helped me to see that I was strong and I deserved to be happy again. He would always tell me one of the biggest things he was drawn to was my strength, even if it was hard for me to realize that I possessed any strength at the time. He helped me feel alive again.

When the time came for me to tell my daughters that I was seeing someone, I knew it would not be easy. Michael was in my life for 23 years and I did not want them to feel that I was replacing their father. I was not. However, what I was feeling for Dennis was more than just a passing fancy, or I would not even have thought to tell them.

During this time, I was having work done to the home I had recently purchased, and there were lots of people coming in and out of the house, including contractors, electricians and plumbers. One day my daughter Jackie went the gym, where Dennis also had a membership. Later, he told me that he saw her that afternoon and spoke to her briefly. That night, I was sitting alone by the fire pit in the yard when Jackie came to sit with me and talk. She told me she didn't like seeing me sitting out there by myself. I thought this was the perfect time to tell her about Dennis, so I began by saying that I had been seeing a particular person and that she knew him.

"You not only know him," I added, "but you saw him today."

She thought about it a moment, then guessed, "X the plumber?"

I got a little chuckle out of that, and we actually still laugh about it to this day.

"Not X the plumber," I told her. "It's someone else you saw today."

After a brief pause, her eyes grew as wide as silver dollars. "Dennis?"

When I confirmed that it was Dennis, she seemed conflicted. Deep inside, I knew she didn't want to see me sad and alone, but it was a very confusing time for all of us.

After telling all of my daughters about Dennis, things got complicated. It was very difficult for them to see me with anyone other than their father, which was all they had ever known. It was like an aftershock following the disaster of losing their father, and a massive reality check for them that he was not coming back. I felt guilty and completely devastated at times because I felt that I was inflicting additional pain on my children, which was the one thing that I was constantly struggling to shield them from.

However, the feelings that Dennis and I had for each other only grew stronger, even amidst the confusion, chaos and pain we were all dealing with. We began spending more and more time together. We talked for hours and listened to music, just trying to find some peace. Each night I would make dinner for everyone. We all seemed to have different schedules, so the days of sitting down to eat at the dinner table together were few and far between. However, sometimes we would all gather at the kitchen island at the same time and share a meal and some conversation, but it wasn't a regular thing for quite a while. Dennis would come over after he got out of work, but his schedule wasn't a typical nine-to-five job. The karate classes he taught didn't start until the late afternoon and didn't end until later in the evening. At the beginning of our relationship, he would always eat before he came over and call me beforehand to see if I needed anything.

It would be the same answer from me all the time; "I'm all set. I made dinner."

He finally realized that it was a better idea if he stopped eating before he got to my house. I really enjoyed cooking and trying new recipes while keeping with my traditional Italian meals. I prided myself on being a good cook. No one seemed to have ever complained, and I would always get "requests" from my girls on what they wanted me to make for dinner.

Dennis eventually learned from my girls that all he had to do was ask for something, and I would make it. Now I get texts from him with a picture or a recipe of a meal and message that would say, "Babe, doesn't this look good?" This is his subtle way of saying, "Can you please make this?"

I have always come through on his culinary wishes, surprising him with the meal shortly afterward. I love doing it. It makes me feel good to see those I care about happy, and if making a meal makes them happy, then I am happy to accommodate, and they are always appreciative.

ACCEPTING DENNIS

Ultimately, Dennis and I did find a true, lasting harmony with each other, but it was a double-edged sword in the beginning. My girls didn't want to be around when Dennis was over. They resented him for what he represented to them; their father's permanent absence for their lives.

Olivia was conflicted about my relationship with Dennis because she really liked him, and was close to him through her karate, but this was a line that had become blurred for her because of my relationship with him. She wanted to like him, but she wanted her daddy back. All my daughters missed their father so much, and Dennis became a constant reminder that our lives were never going to be the same.

It was all too real and confusing for them, particularly Olivia, who was just 12 years old. She didn't know what to feel. At the beginning, and for quite a while after, they all kept their distance when Dennis and I were together. This brought my anxiety and confusion to the highest level. It made me question if it might be best for Dennis and I to just breakup to avoid putting my girls through anymore heartache, especially one caused by me. But what Dennis and I had was special. That's what it always came back to. I couldn't just walk away from him.

I remember a conversation we had at this time. Through tears I told him that I can't stand to see my girls in pain. They are the air that I breathe and it breaks my heart to see them hurting for any reason, and especially if it's something that I am doing to upset them or cause them any more pain.

Dennis said, "You are the strongest most selfless woman I know. You put everyone before yourself, but you have to remember that you can't make anyone else happy if you don't make yourself happy also. Your children want to see their mother happy and healthy. They will see that if you make yourself a priority, they will be happier and stronger for it as well. You can't keep taking on the world alone."

This took me a long time to work through, but I eventually came to realize that the stronger and happier I became, the same began to happen to my children. I truly believe that much of their security lay in my emotional health and happiness.

We endured some very difficult times together, but eventually my daughters came to see Dennis for who he really is, a person that truly loves their mother and helped put a smile back on her face. Ultimately, that is what we all want for each other. We want each other to be happy. We fought through so much together, and despite the difficult moments, under the most harrowing circumstances, we remained there for each other. We may not have always agreed with each other on everything, but we would not break the bond that we have and we did the best we could to keep it in tact and strong.

We are all meant to live life to the fullest, and I believe if we have a chance to be happy, we should take it and not question why we were given that opportunity. Life is meant to be lived and we need not feel guilty for living it. Finding love is a rare and incredible thing and not something to be taken lightly. If you are lucky enough, or blessed (as I prefer to look at it), to find love, you hold on with both hands and don't let go. I know I have been blessed, not once, but twice by true love, and that is something that I will hold onto and cherish always.

Chapter 13   **SLIDING DOORS**

"If you're searching for the one person that will change your life, take a look in the mirror."

I have to look at my life as two separate people. The person and the life I had with Michael, and now the different person I am and the different life I have after Michael. In the beginning, I could not separate the two, and I had no idea how I could be living a new life while at the same time reliving the past and replaying the memories in my mind. I wanted to be able to keep Michael alive through the reminiscences I had and the stories that I told my children so that they would always remember their father. I felt it was important to show my children that we can keep his memory alive and keep our love for him in our hearts while continuing to move forward with our own lives.

For a long time, I tried to "step through the door," moving all of us forward together, but then something would happen, and I would sink back inside a dark place where I felt shackled and imprisoned. It was hardly surprising when I was diagnosed with PTSD, (Post Traumatic Stress Disorder). Some nights I would jump awake during the night from my own screaming and crying. I was literally reliving scenes from the hospital when I was told Michael was gone and or the agonizing scenes of my children when I had to tell them the devastating news. I never knew what would trigger a thought or a memory. There was nothing more traumatizing than the sounds of the tortured cries of my children. Sometimes all it took was someone to make a comment about Michael, whether it had to do with how he died, or a disapproving comment about my relationship with Dennis, or it could have been a day where one of my children was really struggling. Whatever it was, there was an internal battle between these two conflicting parts of myself. There were moments I felt like I was in a trance and I couldn't get the images out of my head.

I felt as if I was trapped within these dark depths of my own mind, like a fighter continually getting into the ring for a bout. I was sick of fighting, and I wanted to surrender and throw in the towel before *the last bell rang*. I would never be able to win this fight, especially if I remained travelling down this path. I couldn't continue to try to numb the pain with the use of any substance. I had to process everything that happened and face it head on, but somedays I didn't want to keep replaying it over and over. Right after Michael passed, I had been prescribed Xanax which I took despite having always hated taking any form of medication. I surrendered to the fact that I needed something to help ease my ever-consuming angst and unbearable anguish in any way possible.

Part of me believes that our society too often relies on medication as a cure-all. I am not saying that medication shouldn't be taken for illnesses, disorders or chronic pain, because these drugs are vitally necessary for many people. However, I also believe that some medications are overly prescribed and dispensed. Unfortunately, when someone is in the midst of catastrophic grief, they want to believe that they can just take a pill and make the pain go away. It just doesn't work that way, as I quickly learned. The pain doesn't immediately subside with the popping of a pill or the downing of a drink, a commonly self-prescribed coping remedy.

ELIMINATING DEPENDENCIES

The inevitable moment came when I needed to let go of the "crutch" that had been there for me since that tragic day in 2015. I depended on this crutch like a friend, though it really was the devil in disguise. I allowed it to take control of my emotions, which it could only suppress, numbing me to a reality I needed to face headlong. It was like being in a classic toxic relationship which you know is bad for you, but you remain in it anyway.

I was trying to run away from all of the things that were causing me to drink excessively in the first place. Half the time I don't even think I was conscious of this. Unconsciously, however, I was certainly trying to suppress emotions I could not deal with. I didn't drink every day, and I never drank during the day, but if it got to a point that I "needed to escape my feelings" this was achieved with a drink. Drinking became a reflex. It was just what I had come to know, but no matter how many bottles of wine I drank, I never found any answers at the bottom of any one of them, and it never helped me escape from reality.

Most alarming of all was the harm I was doing to my children. I did not want them to think that this was the way to cope with problems. If there was anything that I prided myself on it was being a loving, caring, strong, supportive and very present mother.

I could not excuse my drinking and still be all things important to my children, as well as being a good wife and ultimately the person I knew myself to be; the person that I am proud of being.

I was allowing this monster in a bottle to destroy my life, and I knew something had to be done. I couldn't stand the reflection in the mirror any longer. Just when I was beginning to feel that my life was settling into a "new normal" after what seemed such a long time, I didn't know what was making me feel so 'out of control' in my mind? I couldn't understand why what I wanted more than anything in the world, what I had always wanted, was being sabotaged by my own hands. I wasn't going to subject the people that I loved the most to this self-destructive behavior. I had to do something. I needed to be that person I prided myself on being my whole life. Although my recent experiences affected me profoundly, the foundation of who I am did not change, and I have proudly remained the strong, loving person I always had been.

I decided that I needed to get much more intensive therapy in order to process all of the emotions that I was trying to suppress with alcohol. This proved to be one of the best decisions I ever made in my life. I began to regularly see various therapists, multiple times per week. These were professionals experienced in both treating substance abuse problems as well as grief counseling and Post Traumatic Stress Disorder (PTSD). I needed to learn ways to process what had happened to me internally and employ new coping techniques that didn't include destructive habits such as drinking.

I also attended various support groups and met a variety of people who were going through difficult times of their own, including many who had turned to various unhealthy means of coping. Like me, they came to the realization that they were destroying their lives, and they wanted to end that cycle. No one wakes up one day after experiencing a personal trauma and just decides to do things that will completely destroy their life. We all want to change our lives for the better. Many people have a sad story, a tragic event, or some legitimate reason that caused the pain and anguish that they struggle to deal with each and every day. No one has the right to judge anyone else's battle because no one has any idea what it takes other people to move forward in their lives on a daily basis. But in the end, we ALL just need support, love and understanding. Everyone needs these things no matter who they are or what they are going through.

I came to understand that I had been walking through my life "holding my breath." When my life abruptly changed in 2015, it was as if I took a deep breath, (mainly gasping for air) but never fully let it out. I was always waiting for the "next wave to crash."

It was becoming clear to me that I felt like I was drowning at times because I had been trying to control everything. I took everything on myself without ever asking for help or making any attempt to eliminate the things that were causing me so much of my stress. I discovered that when someone goes through a traumatic event, they can very easily get stuck in the stage of processing the event or situation and never get beyond that. The stages of grief have multiple layers that seldom, if ever, progress in a smooth, seamless pattern that you simply pass through like a haunted ride at an amusement park and come out at the other end with your grief complete. We can get trapped in any one of the stages; denial, anger, bargaining, depression and acceptance.

An article I once read helped put this in perspective for me. It was written by Crossroads Hospice & Palliative Care in

2017, and it talked about the popular term *stages of grief* as being misleading.

"There is no path or progression of emotions that mourners follow. There is no timeline. Grief is unpredictable with good days and bad days. It is not a linear process."

The article also talked about *Common Feelings for Mourners*: agitation, anger, anxiety, apathy, betrayal, despair, disbelief, emptiness, guilt, fear, helplessness, impatience, isolation, loneliness, powerlessness, relief, sadness, shame, shock, strength, thankfulness, uncertainty, uselessness, weakness.

With all of these feelings, how could a mourner be expected to "just get over it," "learn to cope," "don't feel that way," "be strong," "let it go,", or "just move on." This is the kind of advice you sometimes hear from well-meaning people as you are going through the difficult process after dealing with a loss or some traumatic event.

In reality, it's not an easy process. However, it is a process, and there is support that one can find to learn to move forward in a healthy way. I have discovered much better ways of coping such as creating new routines and healthier outlets. I have always been one to work out and consider myself to be physically fit, which was why it didn't make much sense that I would destroy all that healthy work I did throughout my life by drinking excessively. I discovered that I don't need alcohol to "cope" with anything, and that in no way did it ever help me cope with anything. It only tried to steal away anything positive in my life.

I am no longer a prisoner to taking Xanax every day of my life. As a result of freeing myself from the shakes and sick feelings from withdrawal of no longer taking them I felt an increased level of clarity that carried over into every aspect of my life. It was like a veil being lifted on all my senses. It was an incredible feeling on so many levels.

What I found most liberating was when I came to realize that it wasn't about me trying to find "the old me" but rather getting to know the new person I was becoming and meant to become. Until I came to understand this, and came to terms with it, I was consistently fighting a losing battle between two versions of myself; one who no longer existed and one that I was desperately trying to become. I then made the decision that I would apply to graduate school to expand on my Bachelor's Degrees in both Psychology and Education and to pursue a Master's of Science degree in Mental Health Counseling. I believe that in some way I can help others that may be going through difficult or tragic events in their lives. I only hope that my story can give other's hope in some way.

REFLECTIONS

All throughout life we look into mirrors. We look into mirrors to check our appearance to see what the world sees, to see what we want to present to the world. Sometimes reflections are not always an outward appearance, but an internal feeling, an interior view of ourselves that may not always portray what we are showing to the outside world. I remember after Michael died, the reflection that I saw in the mirror became less and less of the person I recognized and knew. It had become a tortured soul and I didn't know who or what I was becoming. It makes me think of a song by Christina Perri called "The Lonely." The lyrics are hauntingly relatable: *I'm a ghost of a girl that I want to be most. I'm the shell of a girl that I used to know well...Broken pieces of a barely breathing story. Where there once was love. Now there's only me and the lonely.*

That was exactly who I was for a very long time. I felt I was a broken shell of a person, but I needed to stay strong for three beautiful girls who couldn't handle my falling apart on top of the trauma they already had to endure when they lost their father. I just was not going to let that happen. I was determined to do everything in my power to not allow even a hint to my girls, or anyone else, that I was someone who could not hold it all together, even while I was raging a war within myself.

I recall a particular night early on when I was doing something I often did late at night. I would listen to very deep music that always brought me into the darkest recesses in my mind, while I was drinking, of course. Unfortunately, the result this day was the exact opposite of what I was intending to achieve. While I was trying to numb things and NOT think, I only managed to enhance my depression and bring out every raw emotion I had. This night was exceptionally bad as I had just finished boxing up all of Michael's clothes and personal items. The smell of his cologne was still lingering on some of them.

The next thing I knew I was standing in the darkened room at my mother's house where I had been staying. I paused for a moment, I don't know why, and just observed everything. Music was playing and candles burning. I looked down at one hand that was filled with prescription pills, one that was for anxiety and one to help me sleep, and in my other hand was a glass of wine. Probably on bottle number two by that point. Then I heard a voice in my head telling me, *Take the pills and you can be with him. The girls will be fine. They have people who love them. You are supposed to be together.* I heard this voice as plain as day. When I looked up, I caught my image in the mirror on my dresser. Candlelight was flickering dully in the darkness and all I could see was an eerie reflection of my glazed-over face. Instantly, my own face dissolved and was replaced with the faces of my beautiful daughters. I instantly dropped the pills, realizing that I was fighting for my life, and the fight was with myself. I realized that I did not have it all together, and that's when I decided that no matter what I had to put up with, nothing was going to separate me from my daughter's. Especially not me.

It was a very long road, indeed. Most of the time I didn't like the person that was looking back at me in the mirror. I didn't really know who she was. I created thoughts in my head that weren't even rational. I tried to push away the people that I loved the most, including Dennis. I know it wasn't easy on him, and he could have walked away at any time, but he patiently stuck by me through it all. He knew deep down the person that I truly am, and he helped bring that person back, even though he had to walk by my side through hell in the process.

My children wanted the mother that they knew and loved.

That strong woman that had it all together and could take on the world. I kept trying to find her myself, but every day, for so long, every time I looked in the mirror, I saw a person who was almost a stranger to me. I would continue to fight to search for the person I was before, I knew she was in there somewhere. I sought out a therapist that proved to be another saving grace for me. She explained to me about PTSD, and how this disorder was not just something that traumatized war veterans struggled with. She told me that I was going through something highly distressing, and that the two of us were going to figure out a way for me to work through the debilitating feelings and emotions that sometimes come up out of nowhere. I needed to learn how to cope with these emotions and find somewhere "to put them" without the use of alcohol, which never helps.

It was not as easy as all that, but I slowly began to learn, one small step at a time, how to cope with these things and how to battle my own thoughts in my head. I began to cut back more and more on the drinking until I didn't rely on it anymore to numb my feelings. Before long I found that I could let go of the guilt and the anger that raged within me. This was incredibly liberating. It breathed new life in me and suddenly I could feel the oxygen invigorating every cell in my body and brain. I felt alive. No longer just going through the motion like some automaton. I could see the faces of my children and how they looked at me with a feeling of gratefulness and love. They finally had their mother back. The person who loved them the most no longer had to hide behind anything.

We have scars that will always remain, and there are battles that we will continue to fight, but we will continue to do it together as a family, and get by through the support of one another.

Just recently, I looked into the mirror and the face reflected back was the one I had always known. It was a face that light had come back into. A face that I was proud of. The face was my own. "The face of the girl that I used to know well."

Chapter 14 **OUT OF THE DARKNESS INTO THE LIGHT**

"I am not what happened to me. I am what I choose to become" ~ Carl Jung

Through what I can only say was God's grace, I slowly began to feel the heaviness begin to dissipate. The weight of the anger, shame, bitterness and guilt lifted, and I could actually feel myself not only smiling on the outside, but actually feeling moments of genuine happiness. I was beginning to find my light again and it was miraculous.

It was as if one day I heard a voice inside me say, "You need to let it go. You need to release the anger, the guilt, and not worry about the opinions of those that don't matter. Just keep moving forward." It is something that I have always said to my daughters since they were small, and it is something that they often say, as well. One of my daughters even has it tattooed on her. Some days, of course, words are easier to say than to act upon, but I genuinely felt that with this revelation, everything felt like it was going to be okay. The light had returned. I was so tired of being angry and resentful. I was tired of feeling unconfident and not trusting anything or anybody. It was like a revelation. I wanted my life back. I wanted a life and I deserved to have one and I wasn't going to stop until I truly started to live again. I deserved it. My girls deserved it.

For a couple years we had all undergone so many changes just trying to figure out how to move forward. After all of the devastation, our lives being completely altered, it's been like cleaning up in the aftermath of a violent storm and putting everything back in some kind of order. Each of my daughters have dealt with so many life changes during this time. They graduated high school, started and changed colleges and courses of study, and just continued to fight to remain on a positive path moving forward in their lives. In a time of life when changes occur so rapidly to begin with, not even taking into account the devastatingly painful loss of a parent, it's not easy to always know what is the right thing to do. I only hope that my daughters and I will refer back to the values and beliefs we were raised with to make our life decisions. It is challenging, but in the end it's what helps guide us to a solution.

My girls and I are a team, and we have always been that way. If there is a day that one feels *lost*, we each do what we can to support each other. I watch the girls with each other. The bond that they have with each other is the best gift I could ever receive as a mother. To witness the love shown through their interactions with each other is truly special. They laugh together, cry together, and everything in between. What had been a house of mostly tears and sadness for some time had slowly been rejuvenated with laughter, joking, singing, and dancing in the kitchen. Dennis has become an important part of our lives now. He has become a part of our *New Normal.*

STARTING A NEW LIFE TOGETHER

As time went on my children began to develop their own mutual relationship with Dennis. I believe this is a process that will continue throughout their lives. It is wonderful to see the interaction he has with my daughters. He loves the girls and our family dynamic.

It is definitely a new way of life for Dennis going from a single guy to a household of five and all the chaos and craziness that it brings. He's now part of the daily ranting and the struggle I have to deal with getting the girls to put their dishes in the dishwasher and shut off the lights when they leave a room. However, in the grand scheme of things, these arguments only show us how far we have all come, even as we continue to move forward one day at a time. I myself try to do everything I can to stay in the moment and not obsess about things I cannot control. I try not to live my life in the past, but rather embrace the present. In my life, I have always looked at things as a blessing, and being thankful and appreciative for all that I have. For a long while, I felt I was trying to get some clarity in my life. I was trying to make sense of what I now believed in order to move forward. It's certainly tough to appreciate things when you are consumed by anger, guilt, confusion and doubt, and so many other emotions that consume and eat away at you. Now when I look around me, again I can look at all the beauty of life's gifts that I have been given and I embrace them.

The life Dennis and I share together has endured the twists and turns of this entire journey. Looking back, we have withstood many things that could have easily torn us apart, but we remained by each other's side. He would always hold my hand and tell me to keep believing that things would only get better.

I remember sitting out by the fire pit one night early on in our relationship, when times were difficult between my girls and me. Despite the heat of the fire, I was still cold. I just stared at the flames silently. Suddenly Dennis leaned over and pulled me close.

"In another year from now, things will be different," he said solemnly.

I looked up at him, wanting to believe him, but I was skeptical. "You think so?" I couldn't imagine another year feeling like this.

"You'll see," he whispered. "Time will help to heal. You just have to keep the faith."

This was something I was always preaching to others, but for some reason I was having a hard time of keeping that faith in myself. He was right. He could see the light inside of me even when I couldn't. Deep down we both knew that eventually the darkness would dissipate and the light would finally begin to shine brightly upon us.

It finally did.

THE LITTLE THINGS

Each day brought us further understanding of one another. One thing about our relationship is that we listen to what is important to the other. It's not all about the big things in life. To me it has always been about the little things. In a sense, the little things are big things. He feels the same way. He showed me that

121

he was listening, and he shows me that each and every day. The first time this was evident was when he bought me the porch swing for our new porch that I had dreamt about since I was a little girl. It brought me to tears. He has surprised me with flowers once a month without fail. He knows what I am going to order on the menu at every restaurant that we go to no matter if it's somewhere we have been before or not. I love how we can both do that with each other. On my birthday the first year we were together, along with my gift he also made special trips to purchase a slice of lemon meringue cheesecake from my favorite place that I NEVER eat because I try to watch the calories but I will have it on special occasions, along with fresh and hot McDonalds French fries, which I like to call "evil little incredible things that I can never say no to!" I can say no to almost anything else, but they have a magical power over me.

It wasn't as if I talked about these things all the time, yet it was something that he made a point to remember because it was something I loved. We do this for each other in the everyday things, as well. It's not just something we do on special occasions. I am sure to always surprise him with his favorite desserts or meals. It's always nice to get a surprise text of a song, or a "thinking of you" message during the day. It's just nice to be able to feel that connection and bond. To feel the love inside again is an incredible feeling. It's something we both felt for each other from the beginning, but now it's like a new breath of fresh air has been given to us. It's easy to only be by someone's side for the easy and happy times, and then leave when it gets difficult or uncomfortable, but that wasn't the way it was for us.

The wedding vows we wrote and read to each other reiterated the sentiments of just how special we felt our life was together. We both felt very blessed. It is so special to find true love in a lifetime. I called him the calm in my storm, and the one who helped to bring back the light, laughter, faith and hope in my life. We truly make each other happy, and we just want to share the rest of life's journey together. Somehow our paths led us to each other, it was apparent to us both.

TIME TO BLOOM

A couple of years ago my friends bought a potted weeping cherry tree for me, and the meaning of the tree was for new life. It is one of my favorite trees because of the beautiful flowering buds that bloom in the spring. I hadn't planted it yet because we are going to be doing some landscaping in the yard and I didn't want to plant it only to have to replant it later. I took it inside over the winter to keep it safe from the harsh elements. It survived nicely, but it hadn't ever really bloomed other than a flower here and there and I just figured it would bloom once we planted it. Then I decided to keep it in my office near the sliding door that gets a lot of sunlight and warmth. Just a few days later I walked into my office and gasped because the tree had bloomed incredibly. Flowers were abundant all over the tree. It was breathtakingly beautiful. Here it was, the middle of winter and I have a blooming cherry tree in my office.

I try to find the messages in everything. I believe with the right environment and love we can all flourish. Sometimes we don't know when that time will come, like the cherry tree, that didn't need springtime to bloom. All that matters is that it when it is time to bloom, it will bloom. Same for each of us. I feel like I am like the tree in many ways. I was given new life and light from within. The time had come for the light to shine fully again. It was time to blossom and flourish.

We have undergone so much devastation and trauma, I just want to see us all happy again. While the life that we once had is gone, we can allow ourselves to be happy again. We deserve to be happy again. We can build something new. Something beautiful and fulfilling.

Something I like to call the "new normal."

Chapter 15   **EXHALE**

"Sometimes it's the same moments that take your breath away that breathe purpose and love back into your life."

~Steve Maraboli

Since that tragic day in 2015, I described previously how I felt as if I was walking through life holding my breath. I even had therapy sessions where I was told to literally breathe. In these sessions I was instructed to inhale and exhale fully and shown exercises to help me do that. They said that my body was too tense and my breathing wasn't full, like I was tightening my stomach muscles and holding my breath. I was doing this pretty much every waking minute of the day without even realizing it. Following this unthinkable episode, my body went into a state of shock. I took a deep breath and never fully exhaled.

Trying to understand what my body was doing, I read many different articles on the subjects of anxiety, stress and breathing. I found a couple that really stood out to me.

In a 2013 issue of *Psychology Today*, was an enlightening article written by Emma M. Seppala, Ph.D. It was titled, *Breathing: The Little Known Secret to Peace of Mind. We take our breath for granted but learning to breathe can change our lives.* It stated that: *"We have an intuitive understanding that the breath can regulate our mind and emotions. Most of us have either told others or been told ourselves to 'take a deep breath' when things got challenging. Most clinical psychologists use some kind of breathing practice with patients. However, because breathing happens automatically, many of us don't give the breath as much attention as it deserves nor have we learned to harness its full potential to calm our minds.*

"One of the reasons why breathing can change how we feel is that emotions and breathing are closely connected. A revealing research study by Pierre Phillipot showed that different emotional states are associated with distinct respiration patterns. In Phillipot's study, participants came in and were instructed to

generate emotions like sadness, fear, anger and happiness to the best of their ability. While they were experiencing the emotions, Phillipot's team requested participants to closely observe and report on their own respiration patterns. The research team found that each emotion was associated with a distinct pattern of breath. For example, when the participants felt anxious or afraid, they breathed more quickly and shallowly and when they felt happy, they breathed slowly and fully. Even more interesting was the follow-up study in which the researchers invited in a different group of participants into their lab and instructed them to breathe in the patterns they had observed corresponded to emotions. The researchers literally told the participants how to breathe and then asked them how they felt. Lo and behold, the participants started to feel the emotions that corresponded to the breathing patterns! Several studies suggest that controlled yogic breathing has immediate and positive effects on psychological well-being, as well as on physiological markers of well-being, such as blood pressure and heart rate. Within minutes you will feel better and place your body in a significantly healthier state. The long-term effects of a daily breathing practice are even more pronounced. By activating the part of our nervous system associated with 'resting and digesting' (the parasympathetic nervous system), breathing practices may "train" the body to be calmer. For example, preliminary studies have found that regularly practicing breathing exercises lowers one's level of cortisol --the "stress hormone." Having lower levels of this hormone may be indicative of an overall calmer state of being, which may translate into less reactivity in the face of inevitable life stressors and less risk of heart disease. Although substantial studies of yogic breathing and the brain have yet to emerge, preliminary brain studies of meditation and the breath suggest that they activate brain areas involved in the control of the autonomic system, such as the insula. Control of the breath appears to activate brain regions that guide the parasympathetic, or 'rest and digest,' processes of the body, perhaps thereby inducing its calming effects. Deep breathing has even been found to reduce pain."

What I have come to know and realize is that science shows that learning how to breathe correctly can help you find peace. I actually needed to learn how to breathe again, and I would only learn to do so when I began to let go of so many negative emotions and harmful behavior patterns and began to allow myself to be happy and fully present of mind each and every day. I needed to allow myself to be happy. I needed to allow myself to breathe.

PAVING THE WAY

My relationship with Dennis continued to grow stronger with each passing day. We liked spending time together, especially taking afternoon drives to different places. It was a tradition that began when we were thinking of things to do on one of our first dates. It was a beautiful day and I was driving, which doesn't happen often, even if it is in my own car. I *may* have a bit of a 'heavy foot.' Since I'd rather not watch Dennis grasping onto the door handle with his heart in his throat, I usually defer to the passenger seat and let him drive.

This day, I asked him if he had ever been to a winery. Unlike me he had not. A friend of mine had told me about them a few years prior. It was a nice way to spend an afternoon. Many wineries have very picturesque grounds where you can walk or sit and relax surrounded by nature. I decided to take him to a winery close to where we lived, about a forty-minute drive. We both really enjoyed it so much that this particular winery has become a very special place for us. We visited the winery many times to just sit and enjoy a picnic, but occasionally we tried different wineries, as well. Our lunches would include one particular staple, which was sliced tomato, fresh sliced mozzarella, and imported prosciutto with a bottle of balsamic vinegar to drizzle over the top. For us, it was like tasting a little bit of heaven. Early on, I surprised Dennis with the purchase of a wicker picnic basket for us to carry our lunches. Many days it was like being on a movie scene with our picnic basket, blanket and my little Bluetooth speaker that came with us pretty much everywhere we went. Whether it was the wineries, the beach or Beavertail Park to sit and watch the sunset, our lives seemed to always have some sort of background music, depending on our mood.

On one warm summer day, during one of our afternoon picnics excursions, as we were sitting in two Adirondack chairs and sipping wine under the shade of large pine trees, we watched people setting up for what appeared to be a wedding ceremony. It was so beautiful and picturesque, we both looked at each other and commented how beautiful a wedding ceremony at a place like this would be. It was at that moment that I think we both realized that this is where our relationship was headed. Before then, I had never thought in a million years that I would ever think of getting married again. I felt so many emotions, but one that I couldn't deny was the love that I felt for Dennis. The love that we had for each other. There was no denying that.

We began to talk about marriage more often with each other. We kept it between the two of us for a while because we knew such a thing would prove to be an extremely difficult hurdle to get over when it came to telling my daughters, which we eventually did, of course. It was definitely not easy at the beginning, however. Time did help to smooth out the rough edges that the reality of my relationship with Dennis initially had on the girls. I had always regarded myself as more of a traditionalist, especially when it came to the sanctity of marriage. I had been married at the age of twenty-two and always held my marriage in the highest regard. Always. It was something I believed in and valued. That view hasn't changed. I believe if you are with someone that you love enough to share your life with, the commitment of marriage is a step that you happily take together. I also believe that it is a major life decision, one not to be taken lightly. I know that we were both blessed to find love with each other. To find love again. We both wanted to make that commitment to each other, and we began paving the way on our journey to do so.

THE SURPRISE ENGAGEMENT

We began to discuss in more detail the specifics of our wedding day. We talked about the date and what type of venue we wanted. We decided on a small but elegant ceremony. And since we had spent so many memorable afternoons picnicking, sipping wine, and listening to music at our favorite winery, we both agreed where we would have our wedding. The thing that hadn't been done yet was the actual proposal, including the ring.

Looking at rings and various settings was a daunting task, which I say with complete sarcasm. I enjoyed the process immensely, of course, even though it was limited. I did not pick out the ring exactly. Dennis wanted to know what I liked, so he would have a better idea of the type of ring to get. After all, it would be on my finger each day. And he felt better knowing. Once that was done, it would become official when he gave it to me. He wanted me to be surprised, so he wouldn't tell me when, and it became a waiting game. Even though I knew it was coming, it was still torture. Every time we would go out, I would wonder if that was the day. I made sure I was always dressed up. I tend to dress up, anyway, so I told him he was under strict orders to not propose if I was in any type of sweatpants and sneakers. I said it with a smile and a little laugh, but he knew I was serious.

One weekend we went to New York, and I thought for sure this would be it. Neither of us had been on the Brooklyn Bridge before, the site of so many scenes in romantic movies. As we walked hand in hand along the bridge, I expected him to stop, look me in the eye, and pop the question. But that didn't happen. Knowing that it was coming but not knowing when only made it worse. He had to know it, too, and I figured he was having a little fun at my expense. He just really wanted to surprise me, and he certainly succeeded.

I found out later that he had originally planned to propose

128

on the bridge that weekend in New York but decided against it after he talked to my daughters. He spoke with them first because he wanted to have them involved, and they told him that it would be nice if they could be there when he proposed to me. So together they created a plan, and when the time came, I ended up being completely surprised by something that I already knew about.

It was a warm spring day in April. Dennis and I decided to take a drive to our special winery for the afternoon. Before leaving we also decided to take some nice photos in front of the house. The yard looked really nice with everything starting to bloom. Even the girls got in on some of the pictures. After arriving at the winery and pouring some wine, we sat at one of the picnic tables that looked out toward the front of the vineyard. My back was towards the building and Dennis was facing me. All of a sudden, he put his arms around me and hugged me. I felt him shake his head like he was motioning to someone behind me. When I turned around, my daughters were all standing there smiling. They had their phones in hands ready to capture the moment in picture and video.

I turned back to Dennis, totally shocked as I processed what was happening. He was on one knee with an open jewelry box that held a beautiful, shiny diamond ring.

It couldn't have been more perfect.

I don't know how they pulled off surprising me like that, but they did. I definitely did not see it coming. Olivia later laughed telling me, "Mom, you should have known that something was up because I put makeup on to stay home."

I was beyond ecstatic that my daughters were made part of such a joyous day. It seemed only right we were all together because they were on this journey with Dennis and me and this was something that would affect them also. I know they were happy for me, but I also know that this was a very bittersweet moment, as well. The love I had with their father would never be diminished or erased. However, life was continuing to move forward. But that does not mean that the past has been erased or forgotten. Love is eternal and it goes on forever.

It wasn't always easy to comprehend at times, but it is vital to keep moving forward. It was the beginning of me learning how to breathe again. The smile I was portraying on the outside was finally beginning to match what I was feeling on the inside. I could finally exhale, and I can't even begin to fully explain what it felt like.

It felt like living again.

A NEW BREATH

The months leading up to the wedding were somewhat of a whirlwind, albeit exciting. Looking at the 2018 calendar, we decided that we would be married on September 21. We thought it was a beautiful time of the year, and we just needed to pick a day. I had always loved the song *September,* by Earth Wind and Fire, which begins with the line, *Do you remember the 21st night of September?* What was better than being able to incorporate that song into our day? We were so happy to learn that the 21st fell on a date that the winery had available.

It was set.

Because of the limited capacity of the barrel room (the room where the reception would be held), we could only invite approximately 70 people. Many of our family members and closest friends, pretty much everyone who had stood by us and loved and supported us on this journey were there for us again on our special day. Even my friends from across the pond in England were able to make the long trip, and I was very grateful for that. Sadly, Dennis's mother was unable to attend because a recent surgery did not allow her to do so. She was very much missed, but she was delighted to see the abundance of videos and photographs that were taken by so many other family members who shared them with her.

Dennis and I and my daughters enjoyed planning all the details for a beautiful, elegant wedding that had a *Great Gatsby* flair. The colors of black, white, gold and red adorned everything. My sister and her fiancé fulfilled the duties of Maid of Honor and best man respectively. My daughters were the most beautiful bridesmaids ever, and my not-quite-two-year-old Godchild/Niece Brooklynn was our absolutely adorable flower girl who stole the show, and deservedly so.

The months and days leading up to the wedding date flew by. The summer was a blur with all of the planning that was required. It was exhausting, but it was worth it. When we needed to take a break and unwind from it all, we went out on the water and spent the day on the boat we had purchased the year after we began dating. It was something we did in the summer months whenever possible. I had always wanted a boat, and I thought it was something that my girls would enjoy, something that we could all do together. We had some really fun days out on the boat as a family, swimming, floating, sunning, reading, writing, listening to music. Sometimes friends would meet us on the water in their boats, and we would all enjoy the afternoon together.

When we first got the boat, I had no idea about trailering it and getting it into the water at the dock. I learned pretty quickly, however, and now I think Dennis and I can get the boat into the water and out at sea in minutes. Ours is a type of speedboat with a small cabin, which can comfortably accommodate up to five people.

Dennis is a person who likes his fast cars, boats, and motorcycles, which he has two, but he is a very responsible driver and rarely speeds. On the water, however, every so often someone, either me or one of my daughters, mostly Victoria, will beg him to 'open it up' and go fast. And he does. And fast, it goes. It may sound strange, but just listening to the sound of boat engine is really intoxicating. I don't know who likes that sound more, Dennis or me.

I'll never forget the feeling I got the first time we took the boat out on the open water. The warm sun on my skin, the wind in my hair, and the smell of salt in the air was incredible. It was a complete sensory overload. It felt so freeing. This first experience

I had was so overwhelming that it literally brought me to tears. I felt I could let go of everything that was holding me back from moving forward, the negativity, guilt, anger, fear. I just felt like I could breathe. I just wanted to feel free like that all the time. It took some time to feel that, but when I finally let go of all those debilitating emotions, the feeling was exhilarating.

A new breath of life.

LOVE WINS

Incredibly September 21st arrived. The day that I would take Dennis, the man that God had brought into my life, the man I fell in love with, as my husband. There was a chaotic hustle and a lingering buzz all that morning as my daughters, sister and I were having our hair and makeup done prior to heading over to the winery for the ceremony and reception. Thank God for hairdressers because they have to put up with some serious stress levels. I thankfully have Alyssa, an amazing one for longer than I can remember, one who is more of a friend and didn't even seemed fazed having all these crazy, needy women vying for her attention that day with the objective of making us look like goddesses.

It's funny, and honestly a tad annoying, as I say with the subtlest of eye rolls, how it seems this time in a woman's life is always chaotic while men seem wholly unfazed, going about their business and doing things like golfing, playing cards, watching sports or a movie, even TAKING A NAP. I laugh thinking about the disparity between the sexes on all things nuptial. I think we, as women, put all this pressure on ourselves to have everything be perfect. Naturally, everyone wants things to turn out beautifully and have all of the plans that were made come to a wonderful culmination, but in the end the most important thing is the reason that the day is happening in the first place; the coming together of two people who love each other. That was what I was thinking about all day, especially through all the craziness.

After getting through that morning, I went ahead to the winery to get ready for the ceremony. I was extra excited because I had a beautiful, brand new bridal suite where I could spend as much time as I needed getting ready and relaxing before the wedding ceremony. Although I'm not exactly sure how much a woman can actually *relax* just hours before one of the biggest occasions of their lives. Strangely, I actually do recall being unusually calm. The winery had been working on the new suite for much of the year, and I felt fortunate to be one of the first brides to use it.

Our photographer, Bethany Steere was incredible, and she was really great helping to keep me calm through it all. The wedding photos she captured that day - of my sister, my daughters, my niece and of me putting on my wedding gown and all of us adding the final touches to our hair and makeup - were breathtaking.

It's another 'girl thing,' but I absolutely loved my wedding dress. When I first saw it, I knew it was what I would be wearing on my wedding day. It was something I had pictured in my mind almost exactly. It was elegant, with a 1920's flair, and when I tried it on, I didn't want to take it off. It was perfect. It was as if it had been made just for me and was just waiting for me to come along and claim it.

The bridal suite was towards the front of the main building, so I could see precisely when the guests started to arrive. My daughters would rattle off the names to me when they caught a glimpse of family members or friends as they filed in.

"There's Dennis!" one of my daughters suddenly called out.

As much as I wanted to look, I made sure I stayed away from the window, though not in deference to some silly superstition. I'm a traditionalist, and I just wanted to wait and have the next time I see him be when I was walking down the aisle towards him.

It's time!

I heard someone say these words and I inhaled deeply. The wedding coordinator came and began corralling all of us before leading us down the stairs and outside the front of the building, where we were lined up in preparation for the ceremony. Everyone would go ahead of me, taking their seats on the wooden benches among the other guests. And then I would walk up the aisle toward a beautiful arbor that was decorated with ivory linen and tied back with vibrant red roses. My soon-to-be husband would be standing there waiting to take my hand. The DJ, who had set up on one side nestled within the rows of vines, began the ceremony by playing Pachelbel Cannon in D.

Our DJ, Kenneth Ferrara helped us make the magic of music happen for us the whole night. We spent many hours searching for all of the right songs to play at our ceremony. As easy as that may sound, it was not. It takes a lot of thought and you want to get it just right because music sets the mood for just about everything. At least it does for me. It provided the cue for the wedding party to start proceeding. Erika, Steve and Brooklynn first, together. In no way did we think my almost two-year old niece would perform not only the flower girl duty of tossing rose petals on the ground, but doing so while walking down the aisle by herself. With a little coaxing from her parents, she threw the rose petals ahead of them, adorning the path.

Next came Olivia, followed by Victoria, then Jackie. They all looked positively striking in their long black gowns and carrying bouquets of beautiful white roses. I couldn't have been prouder of them for being part of this day. I know it was bitter sweet for them, but ultimately, they supported and loved me, their mother, who they were grateful to see happy.

Then the music stopped.

Now it was time.

I kept looking down at my beautiful bouquet of red roses adorned with strands of pearls. I think I was trying to keep my eyes on a focal point until I got my cue to action.

134

The way it was set up, we were behind the last row of grape vines and no one could be seen until we came around the corner and headed down the aisle.

Ellie Goulding's, *How Long Will I Love You* began to play. This is a powerful song with chilling, melodious piano notes. This was what I chose to surprise Dennis with when I walked down the aisle.

How long will I love you?

As long as stars are above you?

And longer if I can.

How long will I need you?

As long as the seasons need to follow their plan.

How long will I be with you?

As long as the sea is bound to wash up on the sand.

As I rounded the corner, I caught a glimpse of the smiling faces of my daughters, family and friends, as well as the loving, gratefully tearful expression on my mother's face. It was the look that any mother would have seeing their child find happiness and love after so much personal tragedy. My father's eyes were beaming with love as well as full understanding of why I couldn't have him walk me down the aisle that day. I didn't want my walk down the aisle with my father to be a painful reminder of the walk that my daughters won't have the opportunity to have with their own father. I knew I would not be able to shield them from their thoughts of this, but I certainly didn't want to add to that painful reminder with a visual which would have been captured in photos and videos. I also felt that at this time in my life, it was not so much about anyone *giving me away*, but rather about me giving of myself. Giving myself to love again. Giving myself to happiness and all of life's new and wonderful possibilities. The same possibilities that I once thought no longer existed for me.

Then my eyes met Dennis's loving gaze and I never looked elsewhere until the ceremony was concluded. With each step I took, every breath that inhaled so deeply, I exhaled slowly.

The closer I walked to my future husband, instead of feeling more nervous, I felt calmer, and when he reached out and took my hand, I knew he would never let go. This was synonymous with how I felt about our relationship from the very beginning.

We had written our own vows to each other, which made it even more special. My vows spoke of fairytales. Many people believe love to be like the fairytales they heard when they were young. Unfortunately, real life isn't like the fairytales you hear when you are a child. Love and marriage mean not only loving each other through all the good times but standing by the other through *all* the things that life throws your way.

I believe that God brought Dennis and I together, and together we would create our own love story, our own fairytale. That is real love, and that is what I vowed to him; to continue on this journey by his side, loving him forever as his wife.

I thought for sure I would lose it right after I began reciting the words of the vows I wrote. However, aside from the quiver in my voice, I managed to keep my composure and keep the words flowing. There was the same risk of both of us becoming overwhelmed with heartfelt emotion and tears when Dennis spoke his beautiful vows to me. He managed to alleviate this emotional tension when he spoke of promising to get me McDonalds French fries and lemon meringue cheesecake every year on my birthday. We all got a pretty good laugh out of that, as well as from my niece, who suddenly decided she was going to lie down in front of the platform where we were reciting our vows. I'm so happy that we got a photo capturing that moment. We all looked at her and smiled, otherwise unfazed by the attention she drew. Two other people might have begun to freak out because it wasn't written into their wedding plans, but we thought it was great, and we even have the photo of the precise moment on our living room wall to remind of us of it.

I now pronounce you husband and wife!

These are the words that rang out by not only our officiant, who was incredible, but also by everyone in attendance. She asked that everyone say it together. It was wonderful to hear it pronounced in unison by all of our guests at that moment. It was especially moving because the people that were in attendance were all important parts of so many stages of our lives. It was truly humbling for me recalling all the friendships that I have been blessed to have made throughout my life, including some of my longest friends who, even if I haven't been able to see them as often as I'd like, were there to support me just as they had through so many other moments in my life, both happy and sad.

As Dennis and I turned around to face them all for the first time as husband and wife, they cheered and I felt all the love that surrounded us that day. Our DJ began to play our perfect song choice, Earth Wind and Fire's *September*, and as we euphorically danced down the aisle, followed quickly by my daughters, family and friends. It felt like a new breath had been given to my soul.

In my heart, I knew heaven's bells rang in celebration for us that day. I believe they continue to ring. There was a time when I thought that the last bell rang for me, that the fight was over. A time when all I could do was to just keep trying to remain standing, even though I continued to fall. I was resigned to keep fighting, continuing to get back up, not just for me but for everyone that needed me, depended on me, loved me. No matter how much we feel there is no hope left, we have to continue to find that little bit of strength each day, taking it a little at a time so we can handle it. At some point you begin to stop taking steps backwards and you are reminded that you have a life worth living. Then one day a glimmer of light shines on you and the darkness dissipates. You begin to feel the emergence of yourself again, a person that was caring, compassionate, and strong and happy. It happens.

Within the faith that I clung to, I felt the darkness move further and further away. I began to again feel things that I had always believed. The belief that each day was a gift and within each day we can find something that breathes life into our souls. The darkness that consumed me was replaced by lighter memories and thoughts. Memories and feelings of love and the promise of love and healing. The promise of life which I will always call *Hope* returned to me. And I believe it is there for each of us.

"And now I'm singing along to Amazing Grace

Can't nobody wipe this smile off my face

Got joy in my heart, angels on my side

Thank God almighty, I saw the light

Gonna look ahead, no turning back

Live everyday, give it all that I have

Trust in someone bigger than me

Ever since the day that I believed

I am changed

And now I'm stronger

There must be something in the water

Oh, there must be something in the water

Oh, yeah I am changed

Stronger

"Something in the Water" ~Carrie Underwood

Made in the USA
Middletown, DE
16 May 2019